Encountering the Fundamentals of Music

Encountering the Fundamentals of Music: An Activities Approach for Classroom Teachers

Robert A. Cutietta
Virginia Hoge Mead
Kent State University

Mayfield Publishing Company
Mountain View, California

Library of Congress Cataloging-in-Publication Data

Cutietta, Robert A.
    Encountering the fundamentals of music / Robert A. Cutietta,
Virginia Hoge Mead.
        p.   cm.
    Discography: p.
    Includes index.
    ISBN 0–87484–886–5
    1. Music—Theory, Elementary.   I. Mead, Virginia Hoge.
II. Title.
MT7.C92   1989
781—dc19   88–13858

Manufactured in the United States of America

10 9 8 7 6 5 4 3 2

Mayfield Publishing Company
1240 Villa Street
Mountain View, CA 94041

Sponsoring editor, Janet M. Beatty; production manager, Gwen Larson;
cover designer, Joan Greenfield; text designer/typesetter, A-R Editions;
printer and binder, George Banta Company.

Cover art: *Musical Forms* by Georges Braque, Philadelphia Museum of Art:
Louise and Walter Arensberg Collection.

To the Instructor

This is an unusual fundamentals book. It is essentially three books in one: a textbook, a songbook, and a warm-up book. Each "book" contributes to the students' comprehensive musical learning, and students use all three sections concurrently. Our goal is to help students learn to read, play, and accompany a selected group of songs with confidence; we also hope that this book will provide students with the musical knowledge that will enable them to be successful leaders of musical activities.

The Textbook

This text teaches the fundamentals of music in the way most people learn about music—through *making* music. It does not teach performance, but instead uses performance as a vehicle for learning about music. The instruments we use are guitar and recorder, and we introduce specific aspects of music progressively as they are needed to perform each song. You will not find the traditional chapters on rhythm, pitch, harmony, and the like. Instead, you'll find "encounters" which are performance-based activities that introduce different musical skills and principles. Each new encounter builds directly on earlier ones.

To help motivate students, we've included opportunities for performances. Too often class instruction ignores the power of a group of goal-directed students working together. This book allows students to interact through the discovery and performance of music. From Encounter 3 on, the class can be transformed into a musical ensemble, performing songs with melody, harmony, rhythmic and melodic ostinati, and descants.

Interspersed among the encounters are three interludes designed to help students improve their performance skills. The first offers hints on singing, the second provides tips on playing guitar and recorder, and the third helps students learn tuning and fingerpicking skills.

At the end of the book is an appendix of listening examples from standard musical literature that are cross-referenced to the musical elements best demonstrated in each piece. These pieces can be played in class or assigned as outside listening. We purposely limited the number of pieces to encourage repeated listenings as new musical elements are introduced in the encounters. Through repeated listenings, students reinforce their learning of new musical concepts.

The Songbook

For ease of reference and performance, we've grouped all the songs together and placed them in a separate section after the encounters. This "Songbook" provides an uninterrupted text, so that students are not forced to read isolated paragraphs between songs. The numbered collection of songs also facilitates easier practice; students don't have to hunt through the text looking for the song they want to perform.

The Songbook is divided into three parts. In each part, songs are at a similar skill level, beginning with the easiest and progressing to the most difficult. We have had success by asking students to perfect songs from each part for a playing exam before proceeding to the next part. With many opportunities to repeat the songs, students reinforce, review, and put into practice the key lessons from the text. As further review and reinforcement, students are asked to fill in some of the information that introduces each song (e.g., the key, the dynamics, the form); as the book progresses and students acquire more understanding of musical elements, they are asked to fill in more of the information.

We need to comment on the rhythm syllables used in this book. We are not proposing that these syllables constitute a new method of teaching. Instead, we have chosen to share a system (close to that proposed by Edwin Gordon) that works for us. We believe the success of these syllables is largely due to the fact that they sound musical when performed. Our classes, especially when performing the rhythm raps, treat them much like they would scat singing. For this reason, they enjoy them and are willing to practice them. Vocal inflection is the key to making these syllables work in the classroom.

The Warm-up Book

The Warm-up Book provides daily class exercises for pitch-singing practice. If one exercise is performed in each class period, the class should be sight-singing in three parts by the end of the term. In class testing the Warm-up Book, we found that it actually increased students' singing accuracy and confidence if it was used in every class period. Also included in this section are exercises for daily class rhythm practice.

Making Music

An effort has been made to limit the number of songs as well as the amount of information given to the student. In our experience this focus results in students who are amazed and gratified at their knowledge and level of skill in just one term of music instruction. We feel that this excitement will be contagious to their own future students.

We hope you will enjoy teaching the fundamentals of music in the manner in which your students will someday teach it—through making music.

Instructor's Manual

As a further help, we've provided a manual that includes suggestions for evaluating performance, possible test questions, and some ideas that have proved useful to us in teaching.

Acknowledgments

We thank the graduate teaching assistants at Kent State University who taught from the many drafts of this book and who offered advice and suggestions on how to improve it. They are Pat Athya, Marcia Paladino, Milagros Quesada, Lois Schleuter, and Ann Waters. We wholeheartedly thank the many undergraduate students, too, who were willing to work from less than perfect drafts of this book and who enthusiastically offered us suggestions. Thank you, also, Marybeth Cutietta, for your proofreading and excellent grammatical help.

We would like to acknowledge our appreciation to the following reviewers of the text for their many excellent suggestions: Margaret W. Mistak, Northwestern University; Scott C. Shuler, California State University at Long Beach; Keith P. Thompson, Valdosta State College.

Last, we would like to give a special thank you to Jan Beatty, music editor at Mayfield, for her early support of this project and encouragement and help throughout every aspect of its production.

To the Student

Learning to perform and understand music ranks as one of the most rewarding of all human experiences. It is precisely this experience in which you are about to embark. Through the use of this book you will encounter the joy and feeling of accomplishment that comes from musical performance.

However, this is not a book solely about learning to play a musical instrument. Instead it is a book which uses musical performance as a vehicle for learning *about* music. As you perfect your skills on the guitar and recorder you will also be encountering and using a wide variety of cognitive information about many fundamental aspects of music.

It is this combination of musical performance skills and functional knowledge of the fundamental aspects of music which leads to the main goal of this book: the development of your musical leadership skills.

You may feel that it is not a realistic goal for you to be a "musical leader." Yet, most of you will assume this role at some point in the future. For many, this will mean assuming the role of a classroom elementary teacher. For others, future occupations might be as a recreation leader, church school leader, special education teacher, institutional psychologist, or physical therapist. In your personal lives, you may someday teach your children a song, or help them with their practicing. Who knows, the "boss" may even have you lead a "carol sing" at the office Christmas party! Regardless of where you fit into the world of music, the information and skills found in this book will create a firm foundation for you to assume a musical leadership position which may eventually benefit many people.

The book approaches the learning of music the way we believe music should be learned: through *doing*. But doing is not enough. Music should be performed ("done") with *others*.

The group approach is important in that there is power in the group setting when it comes to the learning of music. Unlike the old saying that "a chain is only as strong as its weakest link," the opposite that "the sum is greater than the individual parts" seems to be at work when learning music. Thus, it will sound better when your entire class of beginning guitarists play together than when you practice alone. Don't be discouraged. Eventually this will change until you will sound as good solo as you do in the group. However those early class experiences are important for you. When your class finally perfects a song, regardless of how simplistic, the entire class will feel a sense of pride and excitement. *Remember this sensation.* This is the feeling that you, as a leader, will want to instill in others.

Obviously we feel that it is important for you to feel this sensation first. This is perhaps the primary reason for writing this book in a "learning through performance" format.

We hope you will enjoy encountering music in this manner. If you believe you will, you will.

Contents

Songbook Contents

MORE SONGS TO SING AND PLAY

Encountering the Fundamentals of Music

MUSICAL ENCOUNTER I
PERFORMING A SONG

Introducing

Steady beat
The difference between harmony and melody
Accompaniment
Reading guitar chord symbols
Guitar string names
Guitar chords D and A7
D.C. al Fine
Lead sheet notation
A B A form

What You Will Need

A tuned guitar or Autoharp (provided by your teacher)

In this book you will learn fascinating aspects of music in the same way that many folk musicians learned about music—through performance. In this first encounter you will learn to accompany a song on the guitar while singing. This is quite a goal for your first experience with music. Therefore, it is best that we get started. To familiarize yourself with the guitar, see Figure 1-1. An enlarged section of the guitar neck shows guitarists where to put their fingers on the guitar to find individual pitches or form chords.

The diagram on the left in Figure 1-2 is called a *chord symbol*. Each circle shows where to put a finger to form what is called the D chord. The numbers inside the circles correspond to the finger numberings in the figure, showing the most comfortable fingerings for playing this chord.

Figure 1-1

An enlargement of the guitar fingerboard looks like this:

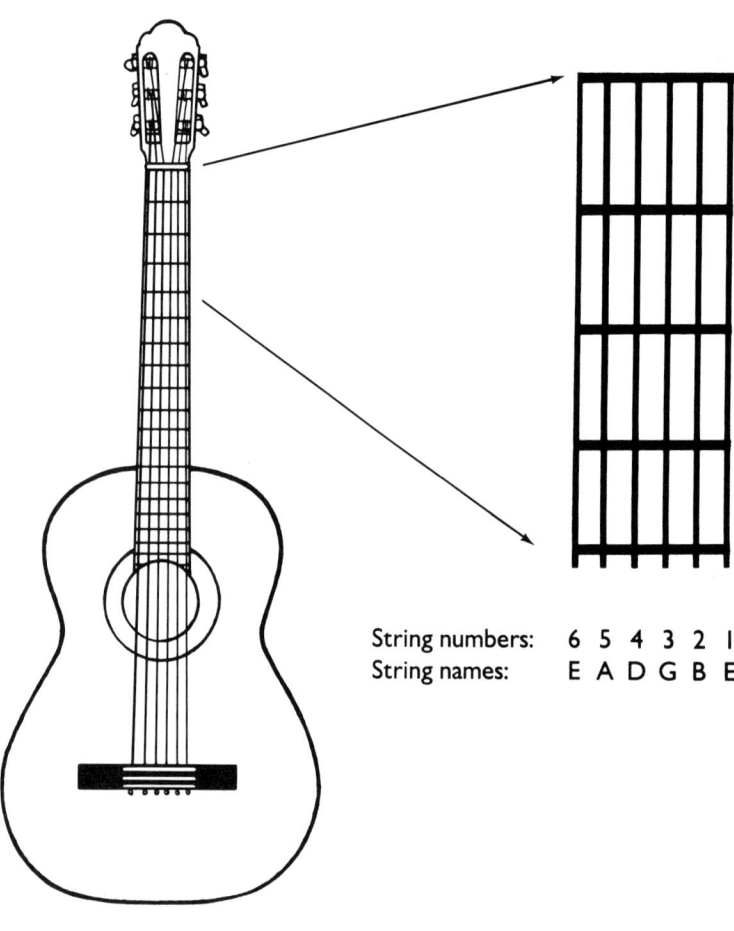

String numbers: 6 5 4 3 2 1
String names: E A D G B E

Figure 1-2

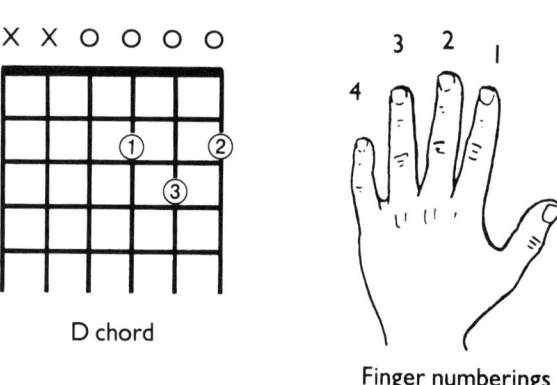

D chord

Finger numberings

Position your guitar on your lap the way you have seen folk and rock guitarists do it. See if you can find the proper place to put your left-hand fingers on the strings.

Once your left-hand fingers are in place to form the chord, your right hand should strum the appropriate strings. Above the chord symbol in Figure 1-2, you will see that strings are marked X or O. Strum only the strings labeled with O.

Believe it or not, you are now ready to play your first song. Turn to Song 1 in the Songbook. Strum the strings for the D chord every time you see a slash mark (/). Be sure *not* to strum the strings labeled X. Sing while you play.

♪ **Perform** ♪
"Row, Row, Row Your Boat"
Song 1

Congratulations! You have just played your first song. Go on to Song 2 in your Songbook for another try.

♪ **Perform** ♪
"Are You Sleeping?"
Song 2

When you perform these two songs, you exhibit three fundamental aspects of music: singing the *melody*, playing the *harmony* on the guitar, and strumming on the *steady beat.*

Playing the guitar would be much easier if the harmony that accompanied melodies always remained constant as it did in the first two songs. Unfortunately, most melodies would also lose much of their beauty with a static harmony. Indeed, the harmony in most songs is constantly changing, sometimes as often as every beat. The performer therefore must change chords many times during a typical song. This background harmony creates the *accompaniment.*

Before you can learn to switch chords, you must learn another one. The second chord in this book is A7 (pronounced "A seventh") and is written in chord symbols as shown in Figure 1-3.

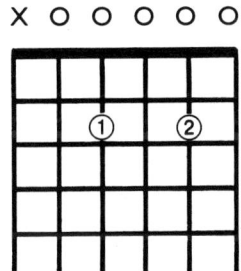

The A7 (A seventh) chord

Notice that you will strum *five* strings for this chord. Practice changing between the D and A7 chords several times, always maintaining a steady beat:

D / / / A7 / / / D / / / A7 / / / D / / /

♪ **Perform** ♪
"He's Got the Whole World in His Hands"
Song 3

Play the harmony of Song 3 by strumming the designated chords on the steady beat. As always, sing the melody while you play.

Lead Sheet Notation

Starting with Song 3 and continuing for the rest of the Songbook, you will see the notes for the melody as well as the words and chords for each song. This format for notating music is called *lead sheet notation*. As you progress through the musical encounters in this book, you will learn more about musical notation. For now, simply follow the words below and the chord symbols above the notation.

The next song introduces an additional piece of music terminology, *D.C. al Fine*.

D.C. al Fine

D.C. al Fine is an abbreviation of the Italian *Da Capo al Fine,* which is translated "Go back to the beginning (Capo) and play until you come to the end (Fine)." D.C. al Fine is necessary because of a common structure of music. This musical structure, or musical form, consists of an opening section, a middle section, and then a repeat of the opening section. Graphically, this structure can be represented as A B A.

The letter A indicates the opening and closing sections, and the letter B represents the middle section. This song form provides a symmetrical and balanced structure that is popular with many composers and songwriters in just about every style of music from classical to rock.

Since the parts referred to as "A" are identical, it is not necessary to print the written music, or notation, twice. By including the term D.C. al Fine, the performer will know simply to repeat the opening section. For example, when you see D.C. al Fine in Song 4, you will need to go back to the beginning of the song and play until you reach the word "Fine."

♪ **Perform** ♪
"Rocka My Soul"
Song 4

What You Have Experienced in This Encounter

Reading guitar chord symbols
Guitar string names
The difference between harmony and melody
Steady beat
Accompaniment
Guitar chords D and A7
Lead sheet notation
D.C. al Fine
A B A form

To Further Your Understanding

1. In your own words write explanations for each of the terms or items in the preceding review list.
2. Read "Introducing Song 3" and "Introducing Song 4" in the Songbook.
3. Practice Songs 3 and 4. Keep the steady beat slow at first; as you become more comfortable, try it faster.

MUSICAL ENCOUNTER 2
PERFORMING ON ANOTHER INSTRUMENT

Introducing

The Autoharp
The Omnichord

What You Will Need

A tuned Autoharp or Omnichord (supplied by your instructor)

In this encounter you will perform Songs 1, 2, 3, and 4 from the Songbook on an instrument called the Autoharp (Figure 2-1). The Autoharp is much like a guitar, except that each chord is "automatically" held down by pushing one button.

The Autoharp can be held either flat on your lap or against your shoulder as if you were holding a baby. Either way, you usually push the chord buttons with your left hand and strum the strings with your right hand. (Some styles of playing differ from this, but this is by far the most common method.) For the most part, any of the strums you use on the guitar can be used on the Autoharp.

The relative ease of playing this instrument has made it popular in school, church, and recreation settings. The instrument does have limitations, however. One of its major drawbacks is that many chords are not on the Autoharp, making it impossible to play certain songs. In addition it is difficult to keep the instrument in tune. An electronic version of the Autoharp, called the Omnichord, has remedied some of these problems while maintaining the ease of playing (Figure 2-2).

Figure 2-1

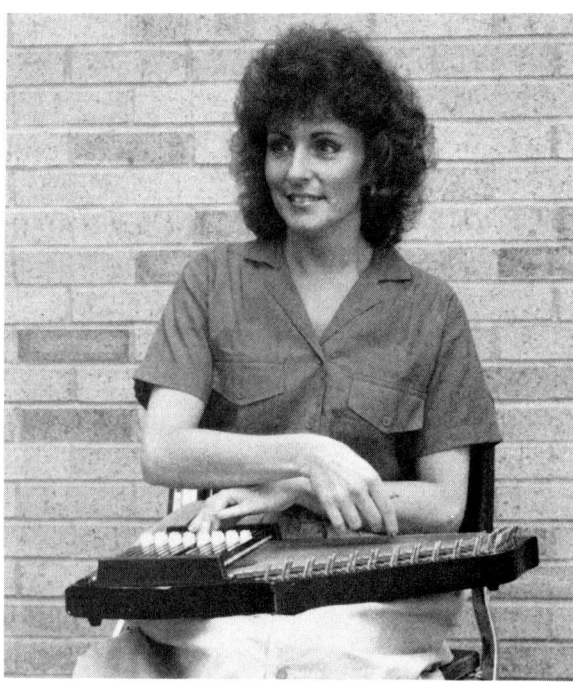

Figure 2-2

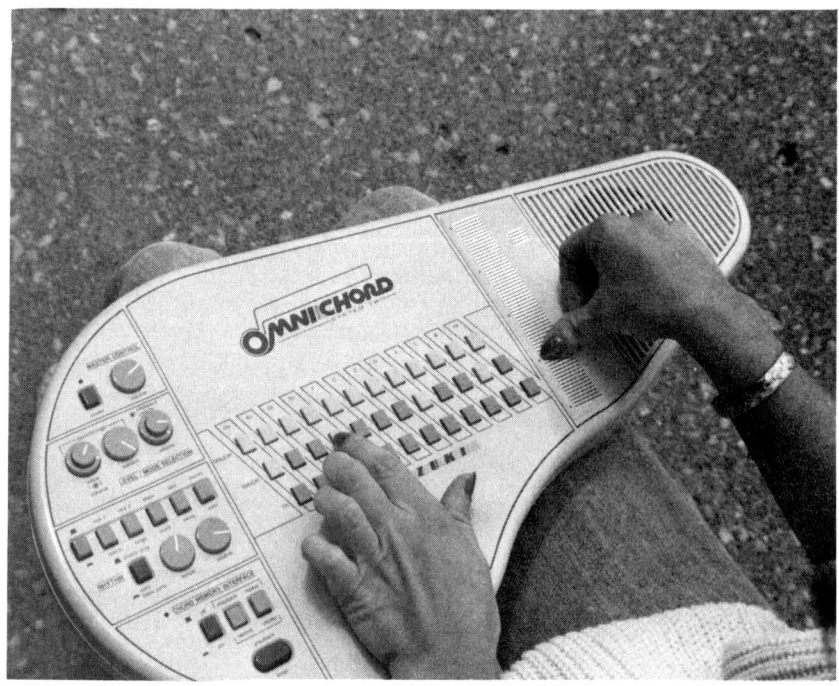

The Omnichord was introduced in the early 1980s and has become very popular with elementary music and classroom teachers. It looks similar to the Autoharp but has touch-sensitive metal strips instead of strings. When you push a chord button, you may strum the metal strips to hear the chord or let your fingers "dance" on the metal strips to create an interesting accompaniment.

Other features of the Omnichord include chord memory, rhythm sections, auto play, and even the ability to play a melody. Some teachers have found the sound from the internal speaker to be less than adequate. If played through an amplifier, however, the sound is good and compatible with young voices. The Omnichord provides a realistic alternative to the Autoharp.

To use either instrument, hold it so that it is comfortable. At first this may mean putting it on your lap so that you can see the buttons. Find all the buttons that you will use in the song. If possible, assign a specific finger to play each chord. For example, if you keep your index finger on the D chord, you simply have to remember to push down your index finger whenever you see a D chord. This will free you from constantly looking at the buttons and will also eventually enable you to hold the instrument upright.

♪ **Perform** ♪

Play Song 1 or 2 on your instrument. On each strum, start at the lowest (biggest) string or metallic bar. Strum away from yourself. You must strum quickly to activate all the strings or bars on each beat.

Once you have mastered these two songs, try one that has more than one chord such as Song 3 or 4. You will probably agree that this instrument is easier than the guitar. However, as mentioned earlier, it is not as versatile as the guitar in the long run.

The remaining encounters in this book refer to the guitar as the primary instrument. Yet it is quite possible for you to complete this book on Autoharp or guitar. Our goal remains the same—to help you learn about music through performing it.

What You Have Experienced in This Encounter

Playing a song on the Autoharp
Playing a song on the Omnichord

To Further Your Understanding

1. Take some time to explore the possibilities for sound on the Autoharp or Omnichord.
2. Play Songs 1, 2, 3, and 4 on either instrument.
3. When you feel comfortable with this new instrument, change the chording on the last line of Song 1, "Row, Row, Row Your Boat," to the following:

   A7　　/　　D　　　　/
   Life is but a Dream _____.

Figure 3-1

Figure 3-2
Recorder fingerings for
the pitches B, A, and G.

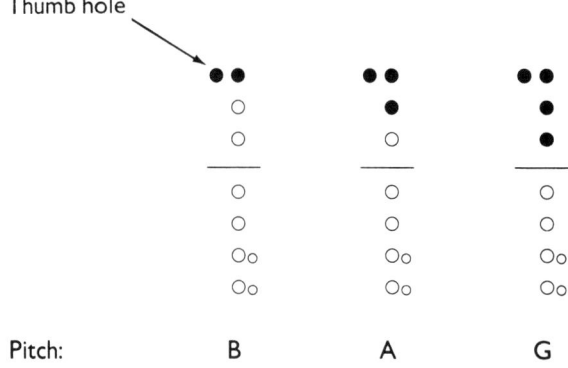

Try playing each of the pitches in Figure 3-2 four times with a steady beat. You will get the best sound from your recorder by forming your mouth as if to say "Du, Du, Du, Du." This is called *tonguing*. To produce a good tone, you must also blow gently into the recorder and support the tone with a steady flow of breath. Take a breath and play four "Du's" on the pitch B. You can increase your breath support by playing eight "Du's" with one gentle breath. With practice, you should be able to play the entire line of sixteen pitches with one breath.

♪ **Perform** ♪

G	G	G	G		B	B	B	B		A	A	A	A		G	G	G	G
1	2	3	4		1	2	3	4		1	2	3	4		1	2	3	4

Ensemble

The next musical experience involves performing on the recorder in a musical *ensemble*. An ensemble is a group of musicians who perform different but complementary musical parts simultaneously. The parts can be performed vocally (choral ensembles) or instrumentally (string ensembles, guitar ensembles, and recorder ensembles). Orchestras, marching bands, and rock bands are also examples of musical ensembles. In fact, whenever musicians perform together, they are performing in a musical ensemble.

For the ensemble you are about to form, some class members will sing and play on the guitar either Song 1, "Row, Row, Row Your Boat," or Song 2, "Are You Sleeping?" At the same time, other class members will repeat the following pattern on the recorder:

Pitches: A   B   A   B   A   B   A   B   . . . (Repeat)
Beat: /   /   /   /   /   /   /   /   . . . (Repeat)

♪ **Perform** ♪
Song 1 or 2

An important aspect of ensemble performance is achieving an appropriate *balance* between the volumes of the different parts. In the previous performance the melody is the most important musical part. Therefore, perform the song again, adjusting the performance volume of the other parts to ensure that the listener hears the melody.

Ostinato

A repeated musical pattern that blends with a piece of music, such as the one performed on the recorder for Songs 1 and 2, is called an *ostinato*. Ostinati (plural for ostinato) are a basic component of musical composition and performance. Examples of ostinati can be found in music from the fourteenth century to the present—in music written for the Renaissance church to music played by "heavy metal" rock and roll bands. Ostinati are a fundamental part of music and will be used extensively in this book.

Play the ostinato for Song 1 and 2 again. It is a very simplistic ostinato, but although it contains only two different pitches, you can make it sound more interesting simply by varying the time relationships, or rhythm, in which the two pitches are played.

Speak the pitch names to the recorder ostinato, being sure to maintain a steady beat. While speaking the names, finger the pitches on your recorder. This is a good practice technique to gain facility with the recorder. Repeat this pattern until comfortable.

Pitches: A   B   A   B   A   B   A   B   A
Beat: /   /   /   /   /   /   /   /   /

Next, alter the timing to say the letter B twice in the space of a single beat. Tap your foot on each beat to ensure that you are maintaining a steady beat throughout. Also try to evenly space the two B's within the beat.

Pitches: A BB A BB A BB A BB A (Repeat)
Beat: /   / /   / /   / /   / /

♪ **Perform** ♪
"He's Got the Whole World in His Hands"
Song 3

Transfer this ostinato to the recorder. Once it is perfected, form a class ensemble and play the ostinato with Song 3. Have some class members play guitar and sing while others play the ostinato. In addition pick one or two members to play a drum on each beat. Pick two or three other members to listen and comment about ensemble balance.

Through this ensemble performance, you have experienced another fundamental aspect of music: the subdivision of the beat. Subdivisions of the beat are the basic building blocks of *rhythm*.

Rhythm

Rhythm is the term used to describe the timing of musical sounds *in relation to the beat*. Rhythm is *not* the same as beat, as is often believed. You have demonstrated the difference between beat and rhythm in the preceding ostinato. As soon as you divided one of the beats into two equal parts (B B), you created a pattern that sounded in relationship to the steady beat. The speed of the beat did not change, but two sounds were heard within the space of one beat. Thus these two sounds were twice as fast as the others. This contrast, the unchanging steady beat and other sounds in relation to it, exemplifies the difference between beat and rhythm.

One way to represent a subdivision of a beat is through the use of rhythm syllables. In the system used in this book the syllable "Du" occurs on the beat. If the beat is subdivided into two parts, as it was above, the syllables "Du nay" are used. Whenever the beat is divided in half (or multiples of halves), it is said to be a *duple subdivision of the beat*. It is also possible to have a triple subdivision of the beat as when you sang "merrily, merrily, merrily, merrily" in Song 1. This phenomenon will be discussed in a subsequent encounter.

Try speaking the following rhythm pattern:

Rhythm: Du   Du nay Du nay Du   Du nay Du   Du nay Du
Beat: /   /   /   /   /   /   /   /

The following ensemble music uses a subdivided beat in the recorder ostinato. It also uses two new musical symbols called *repeat signs* (‖: :‖). These standardized musical symbols inform the performer to repeat whatever is between them.

As a closing activity for this project, try to form a class band to play Song 4, using the parts provided here. You will need guitar players, recorder players, and a drummer. Be sure to assign at least one person to listen for balance.

Parts for Classroom Ensemble for Song 4:

Guitar:	Play and sing Song 4 from the Songbook

Recorder:	‖:	B	B	A	A	B	A :‖
	‖:	Du	nay	Du	nay	Du	Du :‖
Drums:	‖:	Du		Du		Du	Du :‖
Beat:		/		/		/	/

♪ **Perform** ♪
"Rocka My Soul"
Song 4

What You Have Experienced in This Encounter

How to hold the recorder
The pitches G/A/B
Performing music in an ensemble
Ensemble balance
Ostinato patterns
The difference between rhythm and beat
Rhythm patterns
Duple subdivision of the beat
The repeat sign

To Further Your Understanding

1. Practice getting a good tone from the recorder on the three pitches in this encounter.
2. Write a short explanation of each of the terms or items in the preceding review list.
3. Keep practicing Songs 3 and 4 on the guitar.
4. Perform the following practice drills on the recorder, remembering to tap your foot on the steady beat. Notice that in drills c and d, some of the beats are divided into Du nay syllables. Also, be sure to observe the repeat signs.

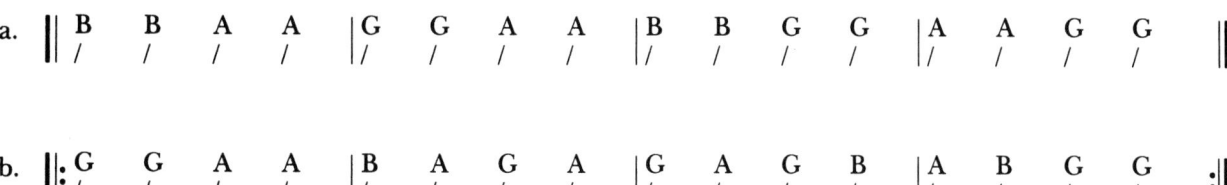

c. ‖: G   G   G   G   A   B | A   A   A   A   G   G |
      /   /   /   / |/   /   /   /

   B   A   G   G   A   B | A   B   A   G   G   :‖
   /   /   /   / |/   /   /   /

d. ‖: B   B   G   B   B   G | A   A   B   B   A   G |
      /   /   /   / |/   /   /   /

   B   A   G   G   A   B | A   B   A   G   G   :‖
   /   /   /   / |/   /   /   /

IMPROVING YOUR PERFORMANCE I

In Encounter 1, you sang the melody and played the harmony of several songs. Since this is a common pattern throughout this book, some observations about singing are appropriate.

You may be wondering, "Why sing?" You might as well ask yourself, "Why speak?" You speak to communicate and to express your feelings and thoughts. Singing, like speaking, is a means for communication and expression of feelings. It is an extension of speech that adds dimension in terms of emotion and pitch fluctuations. The singing voice also is able to express more nuances than the speaking voice.

Everyone has this natural ability. In fact, infants' language and speech development begin with babblings and vocalizations that imitate the sounds around them. Singing or chanting accompanied by movement are the main avenues of expression for the young child. Later, as speech becomes more developed and as the creative expression of song and movement is perhaps not encouraged by parents or teachers, children do not sing as readily. Often, singing occurs only at prescribed times set by teachers or tradition such as in church, at birthdays, when a song leader or teacher leads a song, or for the National Anthem. Many individuals sing only occasionally during their growing years and it therefore never develops into a pleasurable experience.

Some suggestions are offered here that may help you become more comfortable singing and, in turn, learn to enjoy this avenue of self-expression. First become aware of the continuous flow of sound in speaking and singing. If this flow of sound is weak, anemic, spasmatic, and shallow, the singing will sound similarly. You will get out of singing what you put into it. Consider persons you know who command your attention when they are speaking. Listen to their voices and notice their posture, facial expression, and breath support. This is the key! The breath needed to express oneself in speech or song must be supported with energy and vitality. This steady flow of breath can be imagined as a laser beam. As with any physical activity, your singing will improve by practicing in this manner. Keep the following in mind while practicing:

Breath support
Posture
Projection
Pitch
Enunciation

One method for improving breath support is to increase the length of time between breaths in a song. Improving your posture and voice projection will also improve your breath support. These are closely connected in speaking and singing.

Part of good singing is listening carefully to really hear yourself. A good trick is to cup your hands behind your ears as you sing a simple song. Notice that as you open and close your hands over your ears, you can hear the sound of your voice more clearly. If you are not sure whether you are singing on pitch, ask for some help. Sometimes a little help and encouragement can bring back that natural singing voice that you have not used since you were a child.

A song has a text, and the meaning of the text should be expressed through the singing voice or the song will lose its meaning. Try the following suggestions to express the meaning of a song.

- Enunciate the consonants clearly.
- Be sure the breath supply flows through the long vowel sounds.
- Be conscious of the phrasing in the song, just as you would be if speaking. Breathe at appropriate times.
- Be conscious of the mood you wish to depict. You can change the tone quality of your singing voice just as you change it in speaking. Think of the song, "This Land Is Your Land." Try singing the song, changing the quality of your singing voice on each phrase. Always think of the words to help determine how you want to express them.

Singing can be either a social (group) or an individual experience. The goal of an individual experience usually is to "sell" the song to someone else. In this case, the idea of selling is what it takes to perform well. You must mentally reach out to the listener, presenting the song with eye contact, facial expression, body language, and good singing habits. In a group experience enjoyment and successful singing is realized if you listen carefully to the whole group, follow the leader (if there is one), and join in with enthusiasm and spirit.

Whether singing in a group or individually, the best experience occurs when you sing as though telling a story, reciting a poem, or expressing an idea. It all must be done with expression and confidence.

Finally, to become more secure in singing, practice systematically with certain goals in mind. If you can recognize and hear familiar melody patterns on written notation, you will be able to hear how a tune goes and sing it with some confidence and enjoyment. "The Warm-up Book" is included with this text and is intended to be used for that systematic daily practice. It contains fifty-nine exercises with Do Re Mi syllables. At the beginning of the course, it is important to practice only one new exercise a day. Always sing Exercises 1 and 2 every day before the new one is introduced. If you can spend more time on warm-ups, you might repeat some of the earlier exercises. Since you will be practicing the D chord on the guitar during the first weeks of the course, begin the sight-singing exercises on the pitch D, using the syllable Do.

MUSICAL ENCOUNTER 4
ADDING INTEREST TO YOUR ACCOMPANIMENT

Introducing

Measuring the steady beat with stress
A stressed strumming pattern
Communicating the beat pattern
Bar lines and measure
Meter signature

What You Will Need

Your Songbook
A recorder
A guitar

In the first three encounters you performed the steady beat by strumming your guitar and playing your recorder. You probably played the steady beat with equal stress on each count, like this:

Du Du Du Du Du Du Du Du Du Du Du Du Du Du

However, the beat in music is not usually performed in this monotonous manner. Just as language is made up of accented and unaccented syllables, so music is comprised of accented and unaccented sounds.

Stressed Beats

Two stratas of accents occur in music—accents in the rhythm and accents, or stress, in the beat. The beat stresses occur at regular intervals, thus creating a pattern. The most common pattern consists of one stressed beat followed by an unstressed beat as follows:

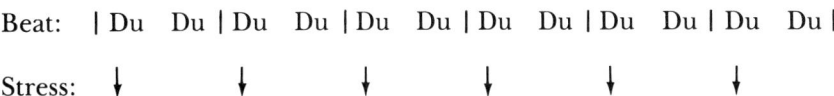

Beat: | Du   Du | Du   Du | Du   Du | Du   Du | Du   Du | Du   Du |

Stress: ↓   ↓   ↓   ↓   ↓   ↓

This pattern of a stressed beat followed by an unstressed beat is very natural; it is related to many of our natural functions such as walking (left and right), breathing (in and out), and swaying (side to side). Almost all music is made up of this pattern of twos or variations of it. This is another fundamental aspect of music.

The following song has the beat measured in a pattern of two. If you picture yourself marching to the song, you will notice that the stressed beat is always on the same foot.

This old Man, | He played One. | He played nick nack | on his thumb

Du   Du | Du   Du | Du   Du | Du   Du

↓   ↓   ↓   ↓

This stress pattern can be used to improve your guitar playing. At this point, you have strummed the guitar across all the appropriate strings for all beats. Try varying this monotonous sound, by using the more interesting stressed and unstressed pattern above. On the first beat, play the strings of the chord with your index finger, strumming downward. Do not play anything on the second beat. Try it with a D Major chord:

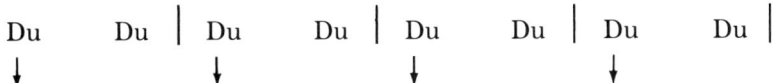

Du   Du | Du   Du | Du   Du | Du   Du |

↓   ↓   ↓   ↓

Once this is comfortable, add the unstressed beat by bringing your index finger upward, hitting the top two strings. To maintain this strum at a fast tempo, be sure to have all of the motion in your index finger, not in your wrist.

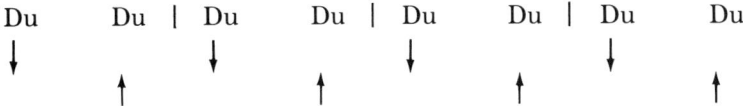

Du   Du | Du   Du | Du   Du | Du   Du

↓   ↓   ↓   ↓

     ↑   ↑   ↑   ↑

You will probably agree that this sounds better and more musical than your earlier strum. This is an example of using your cognitive knowledge of the workings of music (stressed and unstressed beat patterns) to improve your playing.

Some music has the beat organized into a pattern of three. In this case the first beat would remain the stressed beat but would be followed by two unstressed beats. You can demonstrate this on the guitar by playing the following strum. (Remember to "flick" your index finger, not your wrist, to produce the sound.)

An example of a beat pattern in three can be found in "Music Alone Shall Live" (Song 10) in the Songbook. The strum you just played is appropriate for this song.

It is common to combine two stress patterns in a song. For example, if two patterns of a stressed and unstressed beat were combined, the result would be a repetitive pattern in which every other stressed beat is less stressed:

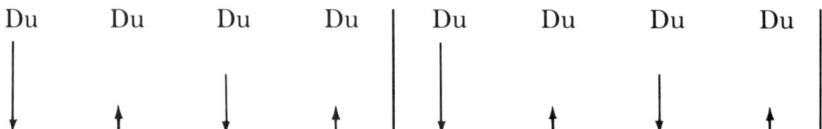

An easy way to imagine this beat pattern is by saying the word Mas-sa-chu-setts. Notice the strong stress on the first syllable and the secondary stress on the third syllable.

For another example of this beat pattern, sing the following song. While singing, tap your foot on the steady beat and imagine yourself swaying from left to right on the stress. Notice that the strong stress is always to the same side.

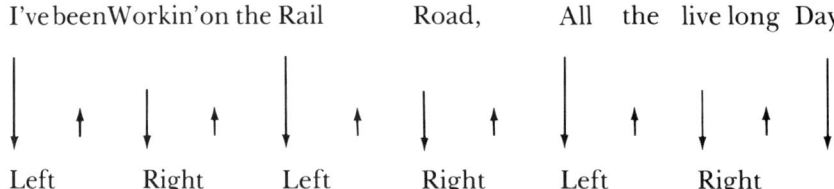

This four-beat pattern creates a very subtle but important difference from the two-beat pattern. The four-beat pattern (with two stressed and two unstressed beats) is the most common pattern in music. Try the preceding four-beat strum on Song 2, "Are you Sleeping?" Be sure to make your strongest stress on the first beat.

You can see that visually notating the beat pattern using arrows would be cumbersome. A much easier method is to inform the performer initially how many beats are in the pattern, then organize, or measure, the pattern by putting lines before and after it. For example, by putting a 4 at the start of the previous example and adding lines to show where the patterns start, the performer will know four beats are in the beat pattern, and they are probably arranged in a strong/weak, strong/weak pattern.

♪ **Perform** 𝆑
"Are you Sleeping?"
Song 2

Thus the previous example is reduced to the display immediately introduced in the following section.

Bar Lines and Measures

In the preceding example the lines indicating where each beat pattern begins are called *bar lines,* and the distance between the bar lines (one beat pattern) is called a *measure.*

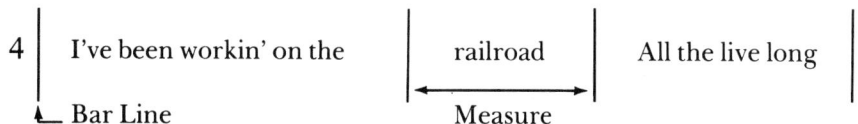

♪ **Perform** *p*
"Jolly Old Saint Nicholas"
Song 6A

As a good example of how stressing certain beats can energize a performance, sing "Jolly Old Saint Nicholas" (Song 6A) in two different ways. First sing it with each beat receiving equal stress. Then sing it over a stressed/unstressed beat pattern. Remember that a beat pattern always begins after a bar line. Therefore the beat after the bar line is the one that must be stressed.

Meter Signature

A number placed at the beginning of every piece of music is called a *meter signature.* It usually determines how the beat is to be felt in terms of the stressed and unstressed patterns. (Threes and sixes placed at the beginning are often ambiguous. This is discussed in a later encounter.) As you have learned, the beat in most music will fall into one of the following patterns:

Twos: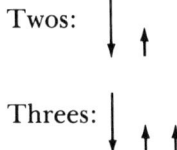

Threes: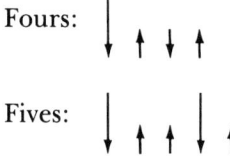

Other meters are possible by combining these two patterns. Meters such as four or even five are stressed as follows:

Fours:

Fives:

♪ **Perform** *p*
"He's Got the Whole World
in His Hands"
Song 3
and "Rocka My Soul"
Song 4

It is important to look at the meter signature and immediately begin to feel a steady beat "measured off" into measures by stress beats.

Before going on, sing and play Songs 3 and 4 and determine how many beats are in each measure. Remember to stress the first beat of each measure on the guitar.

Every musical example to this point has had the stressed beat immediately after the bar line, that is, on the first beat of the measure. This is not always the case, however. It is possible that the rhythm of the music will result in stress being felt in places other than the first beat. This is called *syncopation* and will be discussed in Encounter 11. Further, many rock and roll songs (almost all of which are in 4 meter) have the stress regularly occurring on the second and fourth beat. Unfortunately, our music notation system does not account for this. The only way for the performer to know whether the stress is on the first and third or the second and fourth beats is to know the song or the musical style of the song. It probably seems odd that a fundamental aspect of music such as stressed beats is implied instead of indicated in our notation. The reason is that until relatively recently the stresses were so standardized on the first and third beats, there was no reason to indicate otherwise.

Regardless of the style of music, two aspects regarding the meter will always be true. First, some pattern of stressed and unstressed beats will always be present. Second, the chord changes occur on the traditional stressed beats. Being aware of the stress patterns in the beat (the meter) will help you "feel" when to change.

What You Have Experienced in This Encounter

A stressed strumming pattern
Measuring the steady beat with stress
Communicating the beat pattern
Bar lines and measures
Meter signature

To Further Your Understanding

1. Practice the down-up finger motion on the D chord in a beat pattern of two (↓ ↑) and a beat pattern of three (↓ ↑ ↑).
2. Practice all of the examples of beat patterns presented in this encounter. When a song is identified, be sure to speak or sing that song as you perform the stressed and unstressed beat patterns.
3. Practice these beat patterns on Songs 1 to 4.

MUSICAL ENCOUNTER 5
PLAYING A MELODY

Introducing

Rhythm notation
　　Quarter note, eighth note
　　half note, whole note
Recorder pitches E and D

What You Will Need

Your Songbook
A recorder

So far in this book you have only worked with the beat patterns that underlie music. However, in Encounter 2, you experienced the phenomenon of rhythm in relation to the steady beat. The steady beat was subdivided using the rhythm syllables Du and Du nay. Although these syllables provide an excellent system for learning rhythm patterns, they are cumbersome as a means of notating (writing) rhythm. To be useful, a system of notating rhythm must be efficient and able to incorporate both rhythm and pitch aspects of music.

One system of *rhythm notation* in common use internationally is comprised of notes with two different types of note "heads"—solid: • and hollow: ◦. Usually a note head has a "stem" attached to it, going either up or down: ♩ or ♪.

Each stem in turn can have "flags" attached: ♪ ♪ ♪. Finally, dots can be placed after notes: ♩.

The combination of these four visual elements (noteheads, stems, flags, and dots) indicates how the sounds will relate to the steady beat. As you begin to look at rhythm notation, it will probably look strange. Remember that it is simply combinations of note heads, stems, flags, and dots.

The most common note value in music is called a *quarter note*. It is comprised of a solid note head and a stem as follows: ♩ or ♩. The quarter note most often corresponds with the Du rhythm syllable. Perform the rhythm below in a comfortable walking tempo. Remember to accent the first beat of each measure.

Du   Du   Du   Du   Du   Du   Du   Du   Du   Du

Another basic rhythm note value is called the *eighth note*. The eighth note is made up of a solid note head, a stem, and one flag as follows: ♪ or ♪. Eighth notes are simply performed twice as fast as quarter notes. Eighth notes are sometimes written as single notes but are more often joined together in twos, threes, or more as shown below.

When two or more eighth notes are presented in a row, their flags are combined into a "beam":

Eighth notes are an important piece of notation that are usually used to denote that the beat has been subdivided. Thus the Du nays you performed in Encounter 3 would be notated as eighth notes. Try the following example with half of the class clapping and speaking the syllables. At the same time, have the other half of the class clapping and speaking the syllables in the line at the top of page 25.

      Du   Du nay Du nay Du   Du nay Du nay Du   Du
Beat:

(Remember ♩ = Du)

All of the notes that have been presented so far have had solid note heads. The next three notes have hollow note heads. Hollow notes are held for longer durations than are solid notes. As a general rule, notes that are held two or more beats are hollow; all others are solid. The three common hollow notes shown below include the *half note* with a stem (no flag), which is held for the equivalent of two quarter notes; the dotted half note (a half note with a dot), which is the equivalent of three quarter notes; and the *whole note* (a hollow note head, no stem), which is the equivalent of four quarter notes.

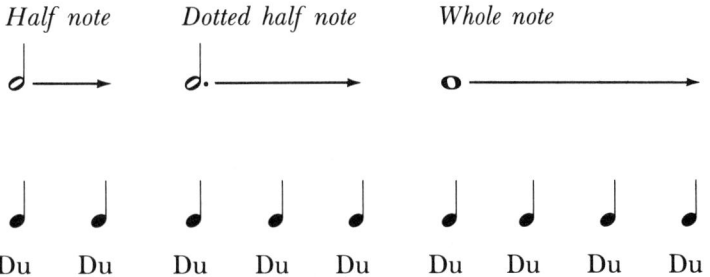

Speak and clap the following example.

Du   Du   Du   oo   Du nay Du   Du   oo

♪ **Perform** ♪
"The Du Nay Du Cakewalk Rap"

You are now ready to practice "The Du Nay Du Cakewalk Rap" (in the Rap section of your Songbook).

You are almost ready to perform your first melody on the recorder from musical notation. First you need to learn two additional pitches on the recorder. These two pitches are named D and E and are fingered as shown below.

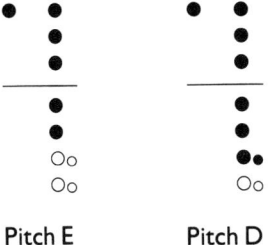

Pitch E   Pitch D

For practice, play the following two measures. For added expressions, remember to perform with appropriate primary and secondary stresses or accents.

E   E   E   E   D   D   D   D

Now look at the example shown below. This example may seem overwhelming because most of what you see has just been introduced in this encounter. However, you will find that you can indeed conquer the task if you follow the steps provided here.

G E E D E G G A A B B A A A D D D G

STEPS TO PLAYING A NEW SONG
1. Review the fingerings you will need for the song. Try each one.
2. Tap a steady beat, and speak the rhythm syllables.
3. Find the meter to determine which notes are to be accented.
4. Speak and at the same time finger the pitch names in correct rhythm.
5. *Now* you are ready to actually play the example on the recorder.

Use these five steps when you practice Songs 5 and 6A.

♪ **Perform** ♭
"Old MacDonald"
Song 5
and "Jolly Old Saint Nicholas"
Song 6A

What You Have Experienced in This Encounter

Rhythm notation
Quarter note
Eighth note
Half note
Whole note
Recorder pitches E and D

To Further Your Understanding

1. Read Introducing Song 5 and Introducing Song 6 in the Songbook.
2. Practice "The Du Nay Du Cakewalk Rap."
3. As always, continue to practice Songs 2, 3, and 4.
4. Draw four quarter notes with the stems going up.

5. Draw four quarter notes with the stems going down.

6. Draw four individual eighth notes with stems going up.

7. Draw four individual eighth notes with stems going down. If necessary, check the direction of the flags.

8. Draw eight pairs of eighth notes with their flags beamed. Notate some of them with stems going down and some with stems going up.

9. How many beats are in each of the following patterns?

10. Practice speaking and tapping the following lines of rhythm. Bar lines have been omitted in items a and b so that your eyes will keep moving at a steady pace across the page.

MUSICAL ENCOUNTER 6
FINDING THE PITCH ALPHABET ON THE GRAND STAFF

Introducing

The pitch alphabet
The grand staff
Treble and bass clefs
Ledger lines

What You Will Need

A recorder
A guitar

Begin this encounter with an ensemble performance that reviews just about everything you have experienced so far.

♪ **Perform** ♪
"Rocka My Soul"
Song 4

Guitar: Play and sing Song 4 on the guitar.
Recorder: Play as follows:

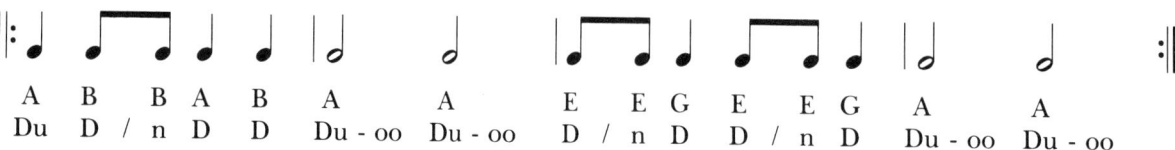

A	B	B	A	B	A		A		E	E	G	E	E	G	A		A
Du	D	/	n	D	D		Du - oo		Du - oo		D	/	n	D	D	/	n	D		Du - oo		Du - oo

The Pitch Alphabet

Musical pitches are named using only the first seven letters of the alphabet (A, B, C, D, E, F, G). Thus the "pitch alphabet" looks like this:

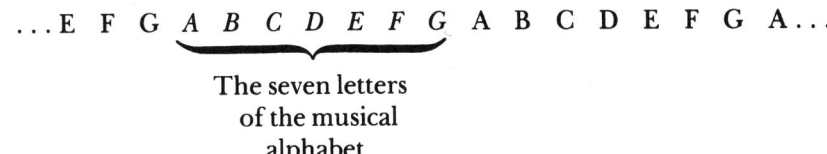

...E F G *A B C D E F G* A B C D E F G A...

The seven letters
of the musical
alphabet

The sounds of these pitches get higher as you progress from left to right.

These pitches were originally written on a *grand staff* of eleven lines to accommodate the highest and lowest tones of the human voice and the family of recorders. Each line and space on this staff represented a letter of the musical alphabet: the bottom line was G, the next space up was A, the next line was B, and so forth.

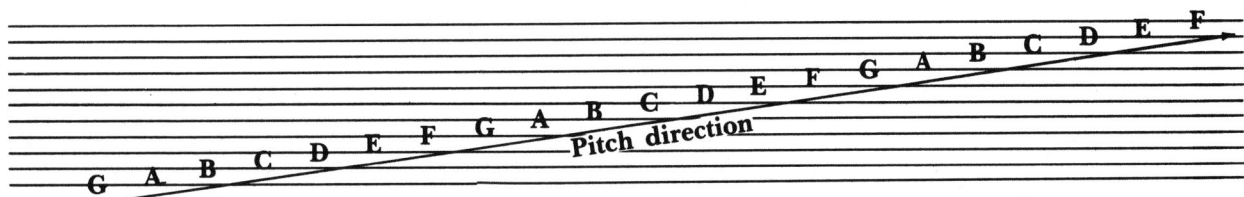

The Grand Staff

Although the grand staff was very complete in its ability to show pitches, it was difficult to read. For example, the notes we have been playing on the recorder would be notated as shown below. To figure out the names of these pitches, start on the lowest line (G) and move up the pitch alphabet (line/space/line) until you reach the notes depicted. You can see that this method of notation was very awkward to use.

Fortunately, it was soon realized that few instruments could play the full range of these notes. To make the staff easier to read, only the top or bottom five lines were used for any one instrument. The middle line was omitted, resulting in two separate staffs, each of which was easier to read than the original grand staff (see the example on page 30).

. . . . . .(middle line omitted except when needed). . . . .

Clef Signs

Even with this change, musicians had no way of knowing whether they were reading from the top five lines or the bottom five lines of the grand staff. A *clef sign* was therefore added at the beginning of the staff to indicate which staff was to be used. The top staff was designated by a *treble* or *G clef,* evolving from a symbol indicating that the second line from the bottom of the staff was for pitch G. The bottom staff was designated by a *bass* or *F* clef, evolving from a symbol indicating that the second line from the top of that staff was for pitch F.

Treble or G clef

Bass or F cleff

Ledger Lines

In theory all the lines of the grand staff are always present. Therefore, to indicate a note that is off the treble or bass staff, simply borrow the lines and spaces that have been omitted from the grand staff. This is done by putting the line through or under the note as shown below. These lines are called *ledger lines.*

Notes borrowed from above staff:

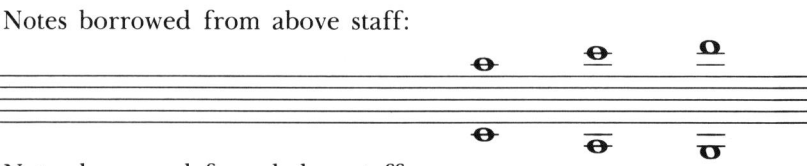

Notes borrowed from below staff:

Both the rhythm and pitches of a piece of music can be notated on the staff. The melody ostinato from the beginning of this musical encounter is shown in the following example.

♪ **Perform** ƒ
"Jolly Old Saint Nicholas"
Song 6B and
"Tom Dooley"
Song 7A

You are now ready to play your first song completely from notation on the recorder. This may seem just a little overwhelming, so break the task into parts by following the steps for playing a new song in Encounter 5. Good luck.

What You Have Experienced in This Encounter

The pitch alphabet
The grand staff
Treble and bass clefs
Ledger lines

To Further Your Understanding

1. Practice Songs 5, 6B, and 7 on the recorder.
2. Practice Songs 3 and 4 on the guitar.
3. Draw a treble clef at the beginning of each staff below.
4. Using whole notes, spell the words below by notating the corresponding pitches on the staffs provided.

A G E   F E E D   C A B B A G E   F A C E

B E G G E D   F A D E D   B E A D

5. Using whole notes, notate the designated pitches on the staff provided below. Do *not* use the same line or space twice.

E   F   G   A   B   C   D   E   F   G

6. Using ledger lines to extend the staff, notate the designated pitches above or below the staff (see the arrows).

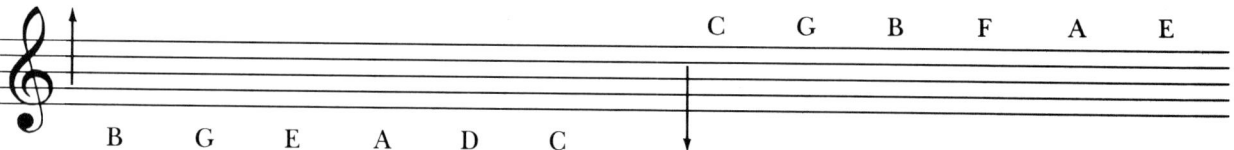

7. Identify the pitches designated on the staffs below.

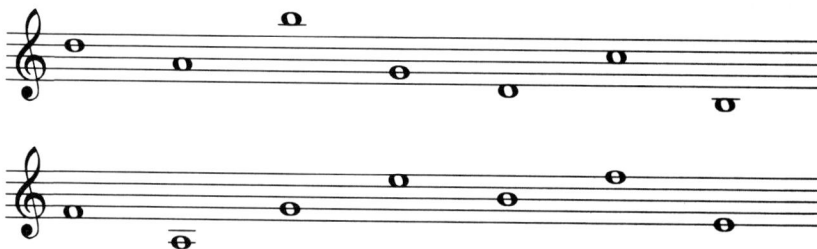

MUSICAL ENCOUNTER 7
THE REST, THE TIE, AND THE DOT

Introducing

The E minor chord (Songs 8 and 9)
Quarter and half rests
Ties
Dots

What You Will Need

A recorder
A guitar

Figure 7-1 shows the chord symbol for the E minor chord. Practice it, being sure to strum all of the strings. Once you can play it clearly, practice switching from E minor to D Major. When this feels comfortable, you will be able to perform Song 8, "What Shall We Do with a Drunken Sailor." Be sure to check the meter signature for the number of beats to strum in each measure.

Figure 7-1

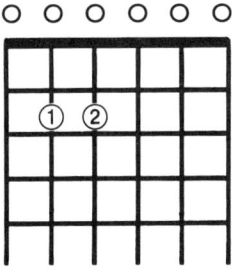

The E minor chord

♪ **Perform** ♪
"What Shall We Do
with a Drunken Sailor?"
Song 8

Since the meter signature of Song 8 is ⁴₄, there are four strums per measure. Thus the accompaniment is like that pictured below.

For variety, try strumming the chords in a half note (♩) rhythm as shown:

When strumming this slower accompaniment, notice that the stress is more apparent on the first beat of each measure.

Song 9, "Tom Dooley," incorporates all three chords that have been introduced to this point. Practice moving between these three chords by playing the following exercise before playing Song 9. Note that the exercise is in ³₄ meter. Always remember to place the stress on the first beat of each measure regardless of the meter signature.

Exercise:

$\frac{3}{4}$ D / / | Em / / | A7 / / | D / / ‖

♪ **Perform** ♪
"Tom Dooley"
Song 9

In Song 9, as in many songs, beats occur that do not have a melody pitch sounded on them. In other words there is a beat and guitar strum but no singing; the melody is silent.

Silence in music is just as important as sound. When composers wish to have no sound, they use a notational symbol called a *rest*. A rest that lasts for one beat is called a *quarter rest,* just as a note that lasts for one beat is called a quarter note. A quarter rest looks like this: 𝄽 .

There is also a rest which looks like this: ▬ . It is called a *half rest,* and like the half note, the half rest receives two beats.

Rests are used to add rhythmic interest to a melody, to add surprise, or to interrupt motion in the melody for a moment. Look for the quarter and half rests in Song 9. Which of the given reasons do you think the songwriter considered when including each rest? Circle the rests so that you will be sure not to sing on that strum.

Now practice the following melodic ostinato to play with Song 9. Remember to rest on the rests!

Another technique used by composers and songwriters to make a melody more interesting is to "hold over" a pitch in the melody beyond one beat. One way to notate this occurrence is through the use of a half note, dotted half note, or whole note, all of which you have already used.

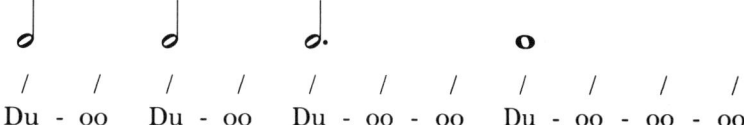

Du - oo   Du - oo   Du - oo - oo   Du - oo - oo - oo

The duration of a note can also be altered through the use of a *tie*. The tie is a musical plus sign that literally "ties" two notes of the same pitch together as shown:

If two quarter notes are tied together like this, the sound is sustained for two beats without being rearticulated or resounded. Ultimately, two tied quarter notes sound exactly like a half note, and four tied quarter notes sound like a whole note.

The tie enables a performer to play many new rhythms. For example, say and clap the following words in the designated rhythm.

Rock   ing   my   soul,   Oh   yeah
Du   Du   nay   Du   Du   nay

If a tie is used to combine the first and second note, it eliminates the word syllable "-ing." The word "Rock" is then held over through the beginning of the second beat, which creates a more interesting rhythm. If the fourth and fifth notes are tied, then the word "Oh" would be eliminated, producing the following rhythm.

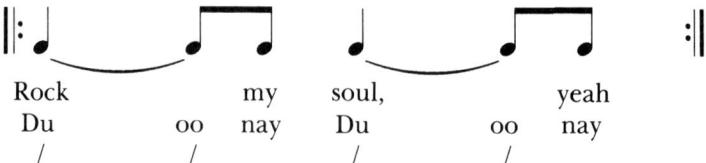

Tap the beat and say the above phrase several times, both with and without the tie. Notice that the word "my" still must occur in the time space between two beats.

A shorthand way of writing the above example is by using a dot. A dot can be used to replace the nonarticulated tied note. Thus the two examples below sound the same.

In practice the dot is placed immediately after the first note as shown below. To find the value of a dot, simply divide the note that is dotted in half.

Another way to view the dot is by its function. The function of a dot after a rhythm note is to increase the note's duration (length) by one-half. Thus a dotted half note gets three beats—a half note is two beats, half of two is one, added together equals three.

In the same way, a dot after a quarter note increases the note's duration by the equivalent of one eighth note.

Du   Du nay

Du   Du (nay)   Du   Du (nay)

Therefore, the rhythm that was notated earlier with a tie can now be notated in shorthand by using a dot.

Rock   my   soul,   yeah
Du   oo   nay   Du   oo   nay

Rock   my   soul,   yeah
Du   oo   nay   Du   oo   nay

In the above example it is important to note that the dot is equivalent only to an eighth note. Therefore half of the second beat still needs additional notes (equivalent to an eighth note) to make up the time of one beat.

The following rhythm ostinato incorporates rests, ties, and dotted notes. Play the beats on a tambourine or any other classroom instrument while the rest of the class performs Song 3, "He's Got the Whole World in His Hands." Feel free to put in the rhythm syllables if you feel you need them; the beats are already designated.

You may also combine this ostinato with the recorder ostinato for "Rocka My Soul," thus making a small band of guitar, vocalist, recorder, and percussion parts. Experiment with the number of performers needed on each instrument to ensure a balanced sound. After some practice you may even want to make a tape of your performance to hear how you are doing.

♪ **Perform** ♪

Rhythm ostinato for Song 3

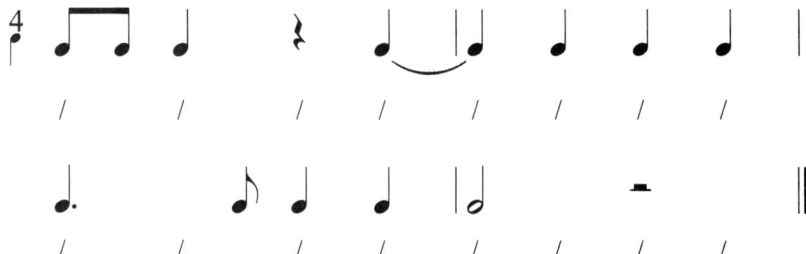

Dotted rhythms add quite a bit of interest to a melody. An example of how effective dotted rhythms can be is Song 22, "Five Hundred Miles." There are only seven different pitches in this song. Yet, because of the rhythmic interest it is a most beautiful melody. You should be able to play "Five Hundred Miles" on the recorder at this point. Later in the book you will learn to accompany it on the guitar.

What You Have Experienced in This Encounter

The E minor chord
Quarter and half rests
Ties
Dots

To Further Your Understanding

1. Add Songs 8 and 9 to your practice schedule.
2. Write in the rhythm syllables for each of the following examples. If you have any trouble, lightly circle in the beats as done in the first example. This will determine the placement of the rhythm syllables.

When you have finished, practice speaking and tapping the rhythms in the examples.

MUSICAL ENCOUNTER **8**
EXPANDING THE PITCH ALPHABET

Introducing

The complete pitch alphabet, including accidentals
The pitches F♯, C♯, D
Enharmonic equivalent
Descant

What You Will Need

A guitar
A recorder
Your Songbook

In Encounter 6 you studied the so-called "pitch alphabet." It consisted of seven letters representing seven different pitches:

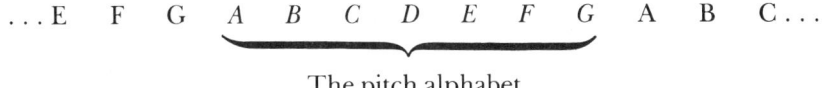

...E   F   G   *A   B   C   D   E   F   G*   A   B   C...

The pitch alphabet

You know these pitches lie on the staff as shown below.

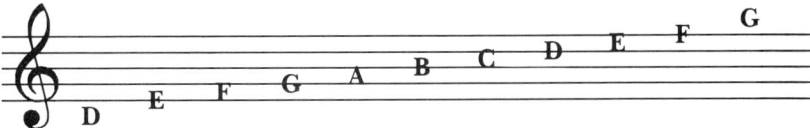

This system works well except that twelve different pitch names are commonly used in music. This creates a problem in that only seven pitch names exist. Since the additional pitches occur between some of the existing letter names, it would be much too confusing to add more letters. The entire staff system also would have to be changed. Therefore, names have been devised, using the existing pitch alphabet, to indicate which pitches the new tones are between. For example, if the pitch is between A and B, it is called either A sharp (written "A♯") or B flat (written "B♭"). When one pitch has two names, it is called an *enharmonic equivalent*. The pitch between A and B has two different names, thus they are said to be enharmonically equivalent. Although cumbersome at times, this system allows more efficient use of the five lines and spaces of the staff.

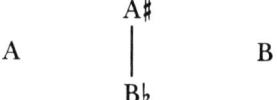

On the staff:

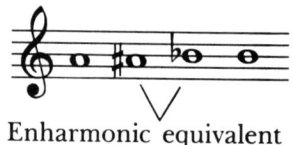

Enharmonic equivalent

The fact that the five additional pitches do not have distinct names has led to the common erroneous belief that these notes are less important than other notes or, worse, that they are harder to play. This mistaken notion probably evolved because the pitches with sharp and flat names happen to be the black keys on the piano. On the instruments you are learning to play, however, they are no different than any other pitch. They are just as important and just as easy to play; they just don't have their own name.

There are pitches between every pitch letter name *except* B and C and E and F. Thus the pitch alphabet looks like this:

...F F♯ G G♯ A A♯ B C C♯ D D♯ E F F♯ G G♯ A A♯ B C...

or the enharmonic equivalent, which looks like this:

...F G♭ G A♭ A B♭ B C D♭ D E♭ E F G♭ G A♭ A B♭ B C...

When all the enharmonic equivalents are listed, the complete pitch alphabet is as follows:

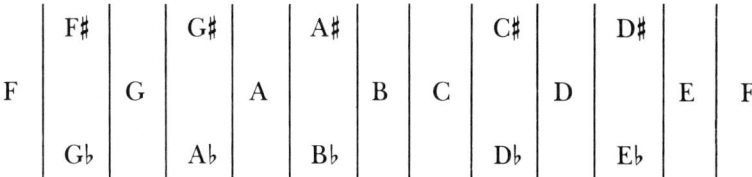

Accidentals

Both sharps and flats are referred to as *accidentals*. To notate an accidental, put the appropriate symbol directly *before* the note, making sure that it is on the same line or space as the note.

In this encounter you will learn to play three new pitches on the recorder. Two of these new pitches are sharps. Again, this does not make them harder or special in any way. The three new pitches are notated and fingered as shown below. Notice that you can now play a high D and a low D. Practice moving from one to the other until the jump is smooth.

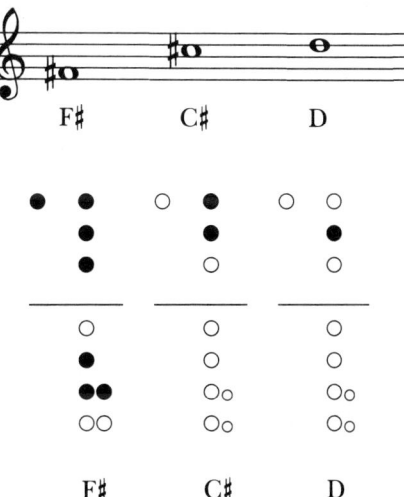

Another interesting aspect of notation can be seen in the following example. Notice that the low D is in a space on the staff, whereas the high D is on a line. This is always the case. Whenever a letter name repeats, it will always appear on the opposite location. In other words, if it was initially on a line, it will be in a space when it repeats and vice versa.

As a fun way to practice your recorder skills, you are going to write your own melody. In item 4 of the To Further Your Understanding section for this encounter you will find the staffs have been divided into eight measures. Three measures are complete; the other measures have only a rhythm written below them. You are to decide which pitches to add to this rhythm. Use any of the pitches you know on the recorder. Be sure to put a sharp before F and C if you use them. Experiment, make changes, and when it is the way you like it, play it for a class member. Ask that person for suggestions as to how to make your melody more effective. Is the rhythm interesting? Is the sequence of pitches logical? Are there any suggestions for improving it? Can your "critic" read your notation and play from your copy?

♪ **Perform** ♭
"Michael, Row the Boat Ashore"
on the recorder
Song 11

Song 11, "Michael, Row the Boat Ashore," uses these new pitches. Practice the song very slowly at first. Some of the notated rhythm patterns may not be familiar to you. Since you almost certainly have heard the song before, play the rhythm you have heard.

Descant

In the next ensemble piece to be performed, the recorder part is not an ostinato as it has been in all of the earlier ensemble pieces. An ostinato is meant to be "obstinate" in nature; as such, it is often not very interesting by itself. In this ensemble the recorder part is actually another melody that harmonizes with the main melody of the song. This type of counter-melody is called a *descant*. The descant for Song 10, "Music Alone Shall Live," is notated in the Songbook along with the song.

♪ **Perform** ♭
ensemble performance of
"Music Alone Shall Live"
Song 10

As a closing project to this encounter, create a classroom ensemble for Song 10 as written in the Songbook. Work to have a proper balance between the melody, harmony, and descant. You may wish to choose a conductor to balance the parts.

What You Have Experienced in This Encounter

The complete pitch alphabet, including accidentals
The pitches F♯, C♯, D
Enharmonic equivalent
Descant

To Further Your Understanding

1. Keep practicing Songs 3–10 in the Songbook.
2. Read Introducing Song 11.
3. Add Song 11 to your practicing schedule.
4. Follow the directions given in this encounter to write your own melody. Use a pencil until the final copy is complete so that changes can be made easily.

5. Write the complete pitch alphabet showing the enharmonic equivalents. Begin on A, continuing past the next A.

6. Write the complete pitch alphabet as you did in item 5, this time notating it on the staff. Be sure to notate the enharmonic equivalents. (For example, A A♯ B♭ B C etc.)

7. Notate the pitches indicated below the following staff. Be sure to place the sharps and flats on the exact line or space as the pitch. Otherwise, they look like they are "floating" in space.

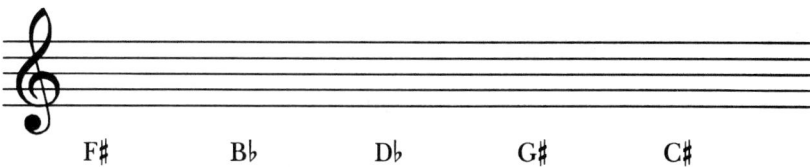

F♯   B♭   D♭   G♯   C♯

IMPROVING YOUR PERFORMANCE 2

As you practice the songs on the guitar and recorder, you can improve your performance by applying some of the principles described here. Some of these principles are applications of what has been learned in Encounters 1–7. Other principles are new.

Practice the following tips with any of the songs you have learned so far. Many of these principles are fundamental aspects of music performance and should improve your sound regardless of the song or even the instrument you are playing.

Guitar

TIP ONE

Many beginning guitarists devote most of their concentration to their left hand. This is understandable in that the finger movements of this hand are new and somewhat awkward for most people. However, it is the right hand that makes the most difference in a quality performance. For example, if you were to play a very difficult chord with your left hand but strummed the chord timidly with your right hand thumb, you would sound like a beginner. Conversely, if you played an easy chord, such as D or A7, but strummed a confident accented strum with your right hand, you could sound like a professional!

The reason that this is true is because of the stress/beat/accent phenomena discussed in Encounter 4. Music listeners expect accents on the strong beats in a piece of music. You can therefore improve your performance on the guitar quite easily by simply accenting the first strum of each measure. One way to achieve this is to strum with the thumb on the accented beats and with the fingernail of your index finger on the unaccented beats.

TIP TWO

This suggestion is related to Tip One. Just as listeners are accustomed to accents occurring on certain beats within a song, they are also accustomed to hearing a song end with an accent. This is much like a reader expecting to see a period at the end of a sentence When a period is missing, as in the previous sentence, the reader feels uneasy. The same is true of music—if the end of the song is not accented, the listener senses that something is missing.

What is odd about this custom is that the accented final beat is *never* notated in guitar music. Correspondingly, it is *never* left out by the experienced guitar player. It is something that is learned by ear. You can improve your performance by simply adding the extra accented beat at the end.

To add the extra beat, look at the following example of the ending of an imaginary song called "The Teacher's Revenge." It is written in ⁴⁄ meter.

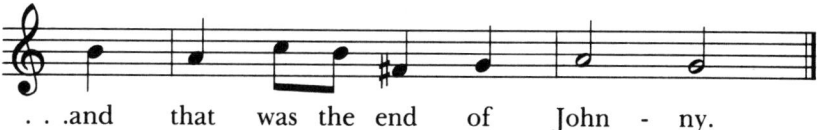

. . .and   that   was   the   end   of   John - ny.

If this song was played as written, the last guitar strum would be on the fourth beat of the last measure, which is an unaccented beat. If the performer accents the last beat, it would sound awkward. Most guitarists would end this song by adding one more beat (technically another first beat) at the end and accenting it. The following example shows how this would be notated.

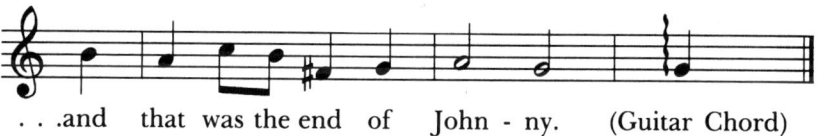

. . .and   that   was the end   of   John - ny.   (Guitar Chord)

Again, it will never be notated this way (except in some piano and band instrument music). It is the responsibility of the guitarist (or the Autoharp player) to put in the extra beat. This rule is not true for melody instruments such as the recorder.

TIP THREE

You may have experienced some buzzing sounds while you practiced the guitar. This is often because your lefthand fingers are not close enough to the fret when forming a chord. When playing, try to have your fingers as close as possible to the metal fret that is closest to the body of the guitar (see Figure 1).

Figure 1

Correct   Incorrect

TIP FOUR

Sit up straight while playing. Try to have the neck of the guitar as close as possible to a 45-degree angle. This will help you to put your fingers in the correct places (see Figure 2).

Figure 2

Correct   Incorrect

Recorder

TIP ONE

A rule of thumb when playing the recorder is:

> More pressure, the higher the pitch;
> Less pressure, the lower the pitch.

Try the following activity to determine the correct amount of air for a given pitch. Put your hand in front of your mouth and blow quickly so that the air from your mouth feels cool on your hand. Next, simply breathe on your hand so that the air from your mouth feels warm on your hand. The cool air technique is closely related to the amount of air you need for high notes. The warm air technique is more closely related to the amount of air you need for low notes.

TIP TWO

A recorder tone is like a singing tone, pure and pleasant. However, sometimes moisture collects inside the recorder and causes the tone to become blurred. To alleviate this problem, place a finger over the hole at the top front of the recorder (not the B pitch hole) and blow quickly. It also helps to swab the inside of each section of the instrument after using it.

TIP THREE

Since the recorder is a wind instrument, it is important to pay attention to appropriate places to breathe in the music. If there is a text, you should breathe with the natural phrases of the text. If there is no text, breath marks (') usually indicate when to breathe.

TIP FOUR

Practice coordinating the tonguing and fingering. Releasing the air should occur in conjunction with the pads (not tips) of the fingers coming down cleanly on the proper hole. The finger should remain over the hole as long as air is being supplied to the recorder.

TIP FIVE

Keep your fingers and wrists relaxed while playing. Relaxation makes it easier to change pitches and makes it less likely for your fingers to slip off the recorder.

To help you maintain a comfortable hand position, it is often helpful to attach a thumb rest to the back of your recorder. A rubber band, Velcro slip, or a standard pencil top eraser can be added to the recorder. For proper location of the thumb rest, notice the location of your right thumb while you are comfortably holding the recorder with all the pitch holes covered. Mark the location of your thumb on the recorder with a small pencil mark. Add the thumb rest at this location.

TIP SIX

Increase your breath support for smoother musical lines or phrases. Choose a song you can play well. Perform it, taking a breath every measure, then every two measures, and later every four measures. Keep extending the length of the breath.

TIP SEVEN

To improve your speed and coordination as well as your tone, try making up melodies on the recorder. First pick a set number of pitches to use (B, A, G, E, and D work well for this). While maintaining a steady beat, play these notes in different orders, always listening to yourself to find combinations you like. Be sure to strive for a good tone and interesting rhythm.

A fun variation of this idea is to work with another class member. Take turns making up four-measure musical statements. Be sure to always maintain the steady beat even between four-measure statements. To someone listening, it will sound like you are having a musical conversation!

TIP EIGHT

When you are learning to play a new song on the recorder, you should follow the Steps to Playing a New Song, which are given at the end of Encounter 3. You may notice that you hesitate, stumble, or do not feel sure of certain places in the songs. When this happens, many people just go over and over the song, actually wasting time when they can use the time more economically and profitably. Mentally (and then with a pencil) circle the places in the music that are more difficult. Try to determine the exact spot where you are stumbling. You may isolate two pitches, but the problem probably lies one note before those two. In other words, back up one note into the problem. Then practice that fragment of the song correctly several times. For example, in Song 7A, "Tom Dooley," you might realize a hesitation in the last two measures. Follow the sequence of practice below to alleviate this problem.

1. Play this pattern five times correctly.

2. Play this pattern five times correctly.

3. Play the two patterns together five times.

4. Play the whole song.

TIP NINE

When you are learning to read music and play an instrument, your eyes, brain, and fingers are so busy translating musical symbols into meaning and moving your fingers from one position to another that you don't let yourself look ahead to know what is coming next. After the initial learning, you should be aware of places in the music where there are several beats of the same note or same chord, or where there is a long note held at the end of the phrase of music. It is very helpful if someone can keep reminding you to look ahead. When you are practicing alone, you should try to force yourself to do that as soon as possible. It is much like driving a car—you know where you are at the moment, whether cars are on your right or left, but you also are seeing a child playing at the side of the road and the light up ahead. When reading music, you can begin early to *read ahead*.

Expression

Regardless of the instrument you are playing, it is important to remember that you are trying to express something through the music. Before playing, read the words of the song. Try to capture through mental imagery the feeling that is being portrayed, then attempt to play the song accordingly. The "Introducing" section for each song in the Songbook has a heading entitled Expression. Read it.

Practicing

TIP ONE

Everyone has heard that "practice makes perfect," yet this is not as simplistic as it sounds. Practicing is hard work . . . and correct practicing is even harder.

You now have seven songs to practice daily. If you are like most people, you will practice the ones you like or the ones that are easy. However, you need to practice all of them.

Successful musicians learn early how to budget their practice time. The first step is to establish a song rotation. You have seven songs now; you will add two more to this list before entering the second part of the

Songbook (at which time you will start working on a new set of songs). Therefore you will want to set up a rehearsal grid as follows:

Songs: \ Days:	M	T	W	Th	F	Sat	Sun
3	X		X			X	
4		X			X		X
5			X		X	X	
6	X			X			X
7		X		X	X		
8	X		X			X	
9		X		X			X
10	X		X		X		
11		X		X		X	

This grid will then tell you which songs you need to practice each day. Further, you will be sure to have practiced them all fairly equally by the time you are ready to perform in Encounter 10.

TIP TWO

Know what you are practicing. Although this seems like an obvious statement, it is often hard to figure out exactly where problems lie. For example, you may find it hard to play the A7 chord with the guitar. The actual problem may be difficulty playing the A7 chord *after* the D chord. It is often the switch from one chord to another, not the chords themselves, that is difficult. Therefore practicing the changes in rhythm may be more beneficial than practicing the individual chords.

One last word of advice: The logic in the old saying, "If you have ten frogs to eat, eat the largest one first," can apply to practicing. If at this point you find practicing some songs to be very hard, then practice those *first*. Playing the songs you like or that you find easy can then act as a reward for working on the hard ones.

MUSICAL ENCOUNTER **9**
MEASURING DISTANCES BETWEEN PITCHES

Introducing

Units of pitch measurement
   Half steps
   Whole steps

What You Will Need

A guitar and two strips of paper ¼ inch wide and about 2 inches long

Encounter 3 discussed the importance of time relationships in music. You learned that most musical sounds are arranged in relation to the steady beat and that these relationships constitute musical rhythm.

Many other types of fundamental relationships are present in music. In fact, it can be argued that music is comprised more of the relationships between sounds than of the individual sounds themselves. For example, the most important aspect of pitch in music is not the actual pitch but the relationships between different pitches. When you play a single pitch on the guitar or recorder, it is simply a sound until you play other pitches that are in some way related to it. From these relationships, you know you are hearing *music,* not just sounds.

Before pitch relationships can be studied, there must be some common method of measuring the distances between individual pitches. Although it makes perfect sense to say that Chicago and Cleveland are 380 miles apart or that the guitar strings are ¼-inch apart, it makes no sense to say that pitch C♯ is 2 inches above pitch A. A unit of measure is needed to communicate distance between pitches.

One system of measurement might be to say that a certain pitch is X number of vibrations more per second than another pitch. A system like this would require musicians to carry calculators wherever they go. Fortunately, a simple unit of measure exists to indicate the distances between musical pitches. The following activity will help you to understand this basic unit.

This activity works better if you work in teams of two. Each team will need one guitar and two strips of paper. Place the guitar on your lap so that you can see the fingerboard. Position one of the paper strips under the strings of the first fret as shown below.

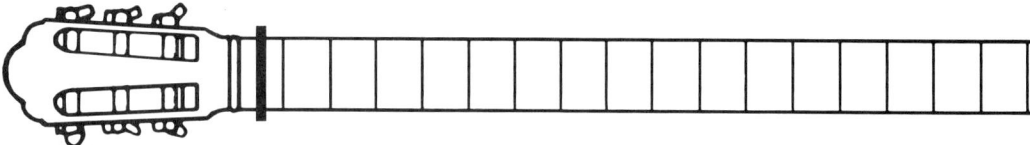

Play that pitch on the largest string by holding your finger down on the string in the first fret and plucking it. The pitch you have just played is F. Move the paper strip up one fret, and you will play the next note in the pitch alphabet, namely F♯ (also called G♭). Move the paper strip up the guitar neck, naming each pitch as you proceed.

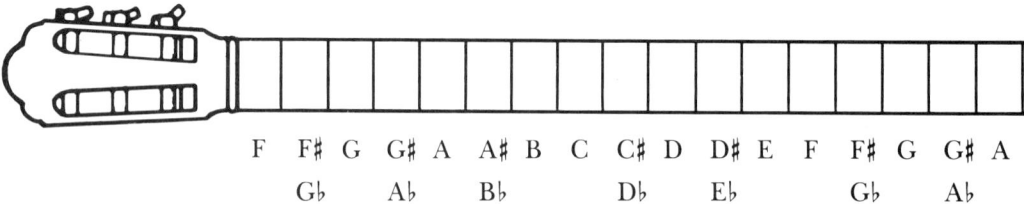

F	F♯	G	G♯	A	A♯	B	C	C♯	D	D♯	E	F	F♯	G	G♯	A
	G♭		A♭		B♭			D♭		E♭			G♭		A♭	

Move the paper strip back to the first fret (F). Take the second strip of paper and place it under the strings on the second fret. Can you figure out the name of this pitch by referring to the pitch alphabet? (It is F♯, or its enharmonic equivalent G♭.)

The distance between F and F♯ is the smallest unit of pitch distance commonly used in Western music. Two adjacent notes such as these on the pitch alphabet are said to be a *half step* apart. Move the paper strips to find two more notes that are a half step apart. What are the names of these notes? Put the strips on the seventh and eighth frets. What are the names of the pitches in this half step? (You should find them to be B and C.)

Half steps can be combined to create the other basic unit of pitch measurement, the *whole step* (two half steps make a whole step). Put one of your paper strips back on the first fret (F). Now move the second strip up two half steps as shown in the following example. The name of the upper pitch is G. F and G are said to be a *whole step* apart.

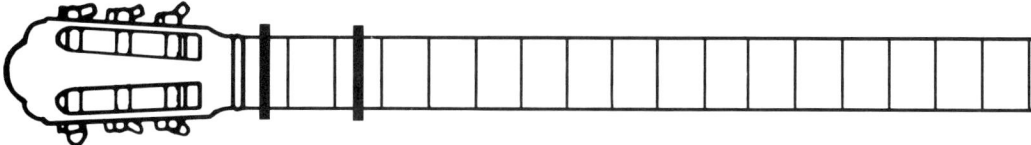

When pitches are notated, it is impossible to know whether two pitches are a whole or a half step apart without referring to the pitch alphabet. Look at the numbered note pairs in the following example. Although all the note pairs appear to be the same distance apart, some of them are a half step and others are a whole step apart. Find the half step pairs.

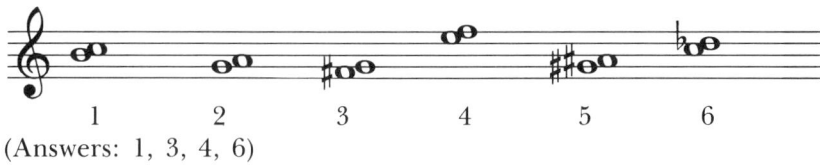

1   2   3   4   5   6

(Answers: 1, 3, 4, 6)

In the example below, notice that the presence of sharps or flats does not give any clue as to the distance between note pairs without using the pitch alphabet. Find the whole steps.

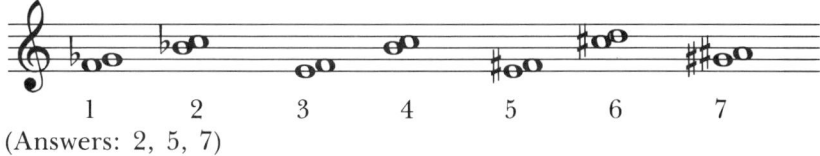

1   2   3   4   5   6   7

(Answers: 2, 5, 7)

The distance between any two pitches can be measured by combining half and whole steps. Leave your strip of paper on the F fret. Now move the second strip up two whole steps. What is the name of this note? (It is A.) Now move the strip so it is three and one-half steps above F. What is the name of this note? (This is C.)

It is essential to know these two fundamental units of pitch measurement. If you are to understand the inner workings of music, you must have a common vocabulary with which to speak. Once you understand these two units you will be surprised at how easy it is to explore both melody and harmony. Many of the subsequent encounters will build off of these two fundamental aspects of music.

On a more immediate level, a common experience for a group leader (school teacher, camp counselor, recreation leader) is to prepare their group to sing a song for an assembly, holiday show, or PTA meeting. Often the leader can make the group sound better by starting the song in a vocal range that is comfortable for the specific ensemble. The leader can start the song on different pitches until the best range is found, and then ask a musician or a music teacher to rewrite the music "up two whole steps," "down a half step," or wherever the group sounds the best. This may sound complicated, but *you* actually will be able to change music in this manner by the end of this book!

What You Have Experienced in This Encounter

Units of pitch measurement
  Half steps
  Whole steps

To Further Your Understanding

1. Continue to practice all the songs in Part One of the Songbook.
2. Identify the distance (half step or whole step) between the pairs of pitches on the following staff. Refer to the pitch alphabet whenever needed. Remember, if the pitch goes up in sound (see the first example), you must move from left to right on the pitch alphabet. If the pitch goes down, as in example 2, you must move from right to left on the pitch alphabet.

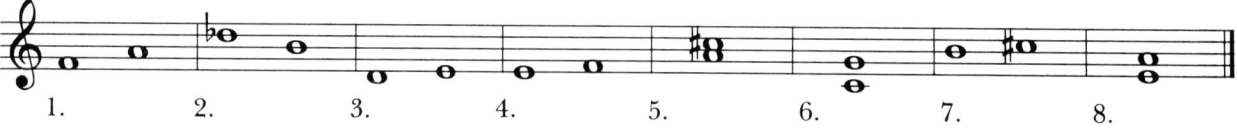

3. Notate the pitches as indicated on the following staff.

1. Whole step above
2. Whole step below
3. Half step above
4. Three whole steps below

5. One and one-half steps above
6. The enharmonic equivalent
7. Two whole steps above
8. Half step above

MUSICAL ENCOUNTER 10
CONSTRUCTING A MAJOR SCALE

Introducing

Constructing a major scale
The pitch distance of an octave
Psychological pitch tendencies in the major scale

What You Will Need

A guitar
A recorder
Eight strips of paper (1/4 inch × 2 inches), which can be found in the back of the Songbook

In Encounter 9 you learned about whole steps and half steps, the basic unit measurements for measuring pitch differences. This encounter introduces one way to use these measurements.

Find the descant from Song 10 in the Songbook. If you were to copy on the staff each pitch in the order that it appears in the descant, without repeating any pitches, it would look like the following example. Do not repeat any pitches; copy each one only once.

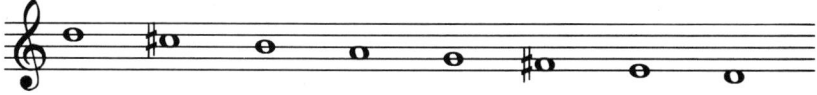

Play these pitches on the recorder in quarter note rhythm. Now play them backwards. Does it sound familiar? It should. This combination of pitches is referred to as a *major scale*. You have probably been hearing music written with this type of scale since birth. You may even be familiar with the major scale and its pitch syllables as shown below.

Do   Re   Mi   Fa   Sol   La   Ti   Do

The following activity explores the make-up of a major scale. For this activity, you will need eight strips of paper (about 2 inches long and no wider than 1/4 inch), which can be found in the back of the Songbook. You will also need a guitar and a recorder.

1. Play on the recorder the *ascending* major scale from above.
2. Play or sing the scale until you are comfortable with the sound.
3. Place the guitar on your lap so you can see the fingerboard.
4. Place one of the paper strips under the first fret.
5. Depress the lowest string by pushing down on the strip of paper; pluck the string. This is the first pitch of the scale you are going to build. Call it Do.
6. Simply by listening, see if you can find the next note of the scale (Re) without switching strings. Place a piece of paper on that fret.
7. Continue this procedure until you have found all eight notes of the scale (Do, Re, Mi, Fa, Sol, La, Ti, Do). If you have found all the correct notes, your guitar neck should look like the one pictured here.

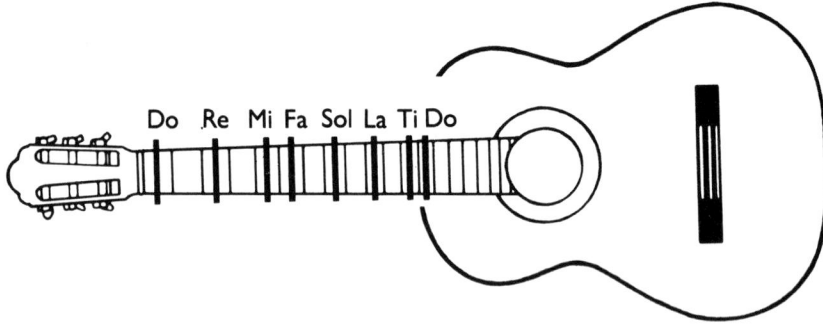

Notice that the pitches of a major scale are not equally spaced. Some pitches are adjacent and others have one pitch between them. In other words, some pitches are a half step apart and some a whole step. The following syllable scale indicates which pitches are a half step apart (H).

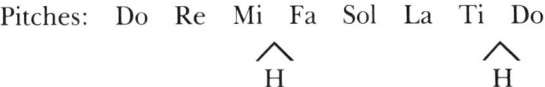

The following number scale indicates which pitches are a whole step apart (W):

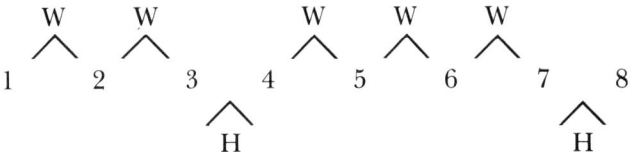

Whenever a combination of eight pitches are arranged in this formula of whole and half steps, they will sound like a major scale. To prove this, play the scale that you constructed on your guitar three times. Each time you play it, start on a different string. You will find that no matter which string you play, the arrangement of pitches will sound like a major scale. This is because the relationship between the pitches, not the pitches themselves, defines a scale. In fact, a scale is defined as an arranged order of rising pitches.

The specific arrangement of pitches just described is only one type of scale, the major scale. Many other possible arrangements of rising pitches exist. In this book only two types are introduced: major and minor scales.

Regardless of the type, each scale is identified by the note it starts on. If it is a major scale that starts on a D pitch, it is called the D major scale; if it starts on G, it is called the G major scale.

A scale can also be constructed on a staff by following three steps (refer to the pitch alphabet as needed):

1. For this example, an F major scale will be constructed. Place Do on the staff. This is easily found because it is the name of the scale.

F major scale

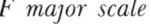

2. Place seven more notes on the staff, being sure to place one on every line and space as shown.

F major scale

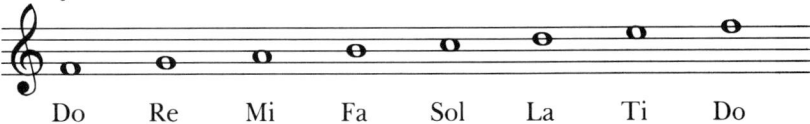

3. Make the pitches match the major scale formula by applying accidentals according to the pitch alphabet.

F major scale

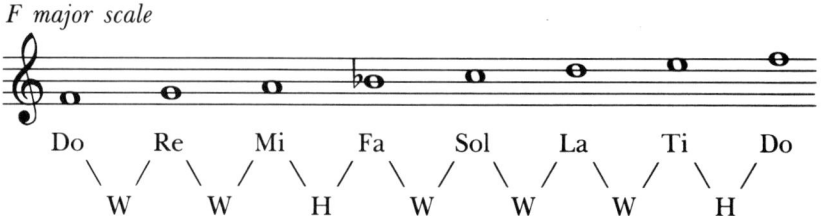

The pitch alphabet:

F	F♯ / B♭	G	G♯ / A♭	A	A♯ / B♭	B	C	C♯ / D♭	D	D♯ / E♭	E

If you look at the F major scale, you will see that the pitch for Fa could be named either A♯ or the enharmonic B♭. In this case the B♭ is chosen because a pitch already has used the letter A. When constructing scales, never repeat a pitch letter. If you follow this simple rule, you will automatically choose the correct enharmonic.

Any major scale can be constructed by following the three steps just given. The only aspect that changes is the starting pitch (Do). If the other pitches are in the proper relationship to it, the result is a major scale.

Notice that both the top and bottom pitches of a scale have the same letter name. The distance between these two pitches is called an *octave*. The distance between *any* two occurrences of a pitch name on the pitch alphabet is called an octave.

Psychological Pitch Tendencies in the Major Scale

This encounter has introduced the relationships that comprise the major scale. However, the importance of these relationships has not been covered. When pitches are arranged in the relationships described in this encounter, they seem to take on individual characteristics, which in turn convert a series of pitches into something that makes sense to the listener.

For example, if you play the pitches of any major scale and stop on pitch Ti, you will feel a strong "tendency" to play Do. This tendency and the others described here is what sustains our interest from start to finish of a song. Whenever you hear Ti, you subconsciously expect to hear Do. Sometimes the expectation is fulfilled, sometimes it is not. It is this feeling of expectation, and its subsequent resolution or nonresolution, that invokes our response to music.

Another tendency in music is that Re pulls to Do. As an example of the pulling power of certain scale degrees, sing the final line of "The Star Spangled Banner" omitting the word "brave."

Sing: "Land of the free, and the home of the . . . "

The last word in the example ("the") is on Re of the scale. Do you feel the strong tendency toward Do?

The apparent pulling tendencies in the major scale are shown in the following example. You can see that Do is a point of rest in the scale. When the pitches with pulling tendencies are followed by Do, they are said to have *resolved*. It is this resolution, or delay of resolution, that makes music interesting.

Re pulls to Do
Ti pulls to Do
Fa pulls to Mi
Sol pulls to Do

Do Re Mi Fa Sol La Ti Do

No one is sure why these tendencies are apparent in the major scale. Most music psychologists believe they are the result of a lifetime of hearing music written in this style. Whatever the reason, they are powerful forces that songwriters and successful music leaders can learn to harness to make musical experiences more meaningful for listeners.

What You Have Experienced in This Encounter

Hearing and constructing a major scale
The pitch distance of an octave
Psychological pitch tendencies in the major scale

To Further Your Understanding

1. Continue to practice the songs on your rehearsal grid.
2. Using the pitch alphabet, spell a major scale that begins on each of the following pitches. Then notate each one on the corresponding staff.

A _____

E _____

C _____

B♭ _____

G _____

F _____

3. Name and notate the pitch that is one octave above (or below) each of the following examples. The arrows indicate whether the octave above ↑ or below ↓ is required.

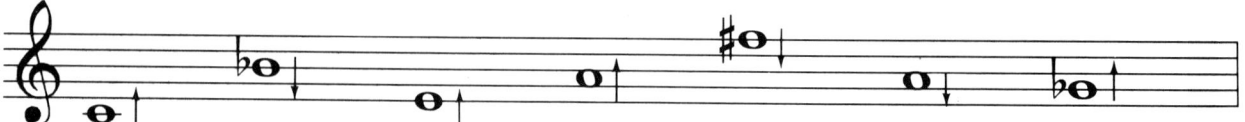

4. Notate the E♭ major scale on the following staff. Then explain why you used an A♭ instead of a G♯ in the scale.

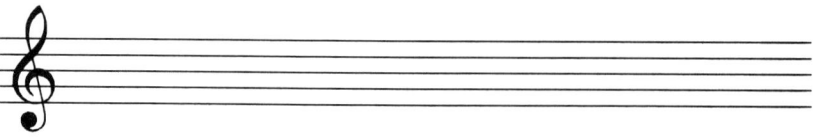

MUSICAL ENCOUNTER 11
SYNCOPATED RHYTHM

Introducing

Syncopated rhythms
Counting the beats in a measure
Lower part of meter signature
The G chord on the guitar

What You Will Need

A recorder
A guitar

You have already learned in a previous encounter that ties, dots, and rests add rhythmic interest to a melody. This encounter explores another very common aspect of rhythm called *syncopation*. To fully appreciate the phenomenon of syncopation, it would be helpful to understand beats in terms of their importance within a measure. You have been speaking the syllable Du on every beat and the syllables Du nay whenever the beat was divided. When you spoke the beats, it was the dynamics of your voice that determined the stressed and unstressed beats in the measure. A more reliable way to realize the importance of each beat is to count them. Compare the following two ways of speaking a rhythm pattern. Be sure to feel the stress on the downbeat of the measure.

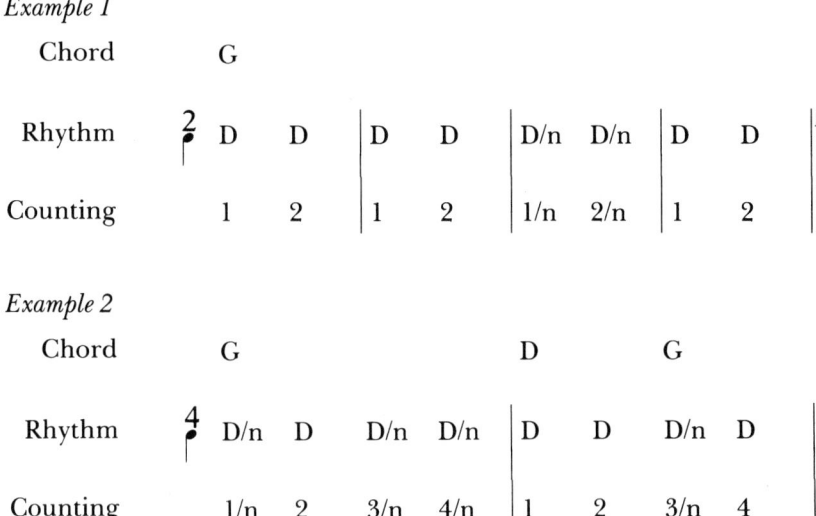

Example 1

Chord	G							
Rhythm	⅔ D	D	D	D	D/n	D/n	D	D
Counting	1	2	1	2	1/n	2/n	1	2

Example 2

Chord	G				D	G		
Rhythm	4/4 D/n	D	D/n	D/n	D	D	D/n	D
Counting	1/n	2	3/n	4/n	1	2	3/n	4

Whenever performing music, the downbeat, or first beat of the measure, generally is stressed. The beat that follows is somewhat relaxed and is a preparation for the next stressed beat. (Notice the difference, however, when there are three beats in a measure.)

Whenever there are two beats per measure as in part A below, beat 1 is stressed, beat 2 is unstressed. Whenever there are three beats per measure as in part B, beat 1 is stressed; beats 2 and 3 are unstressed. Whenever there are four beats in a measure as in part C, beats 1 and 3 are stressed; beats 2 and 4 are unstressed.

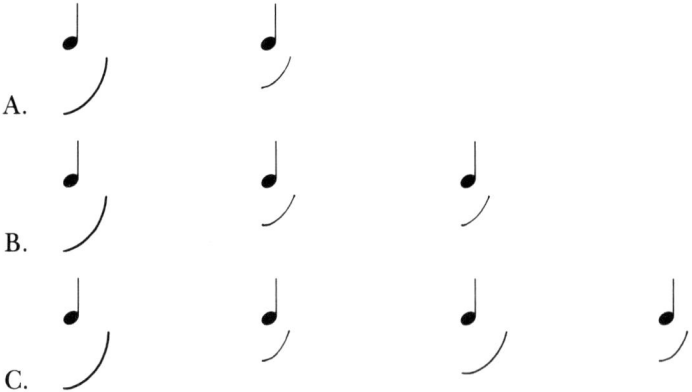

Go back and repeat Examples 1 and 2, strumming the beats on the guitar. Since you will need the G chord later in this encounter, find it on the guitar with the help of Figure 11-1, and then play and count the same two examples. The G chord uses all six strings on the guitar, so you can concentrate on the rhythm activity of counting instead of which strings to strum.

Figure 11-1

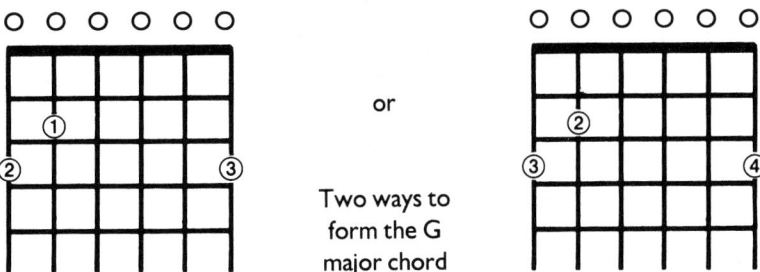

or

Two ways to form the G major chord

From now on, it would be wise to perform all rhythms both with the relaxed sound of "Du" and "Du nay" and also with the appropriate counting of beats. In the Songbook, there is a rhythm rap called "The Du Nay Du Cakewalk." It is meant for practice but with a little ingenuity on your part, it can take on the spirit of a fun composition. Guitar chords have been included, but be sure you can speak and tap the rhythm well before you add the guitar accompaniment.

♪ **Perform** ♪
"The Du Nay Du Cakewalk"

As you look at more difficult rhythms, remember that the numbers only substitute for the Du syllable. Think of the Du as the initial sound of the beat. The relaxed sound of the "nay" is still to be used when the beat is divided. Here are two examples for you to study and, more importantly, to speak and tap. Example 1 is the rhythm ostinato that you performed with the song "He's Got the Whole World in His Hands."

Example 1

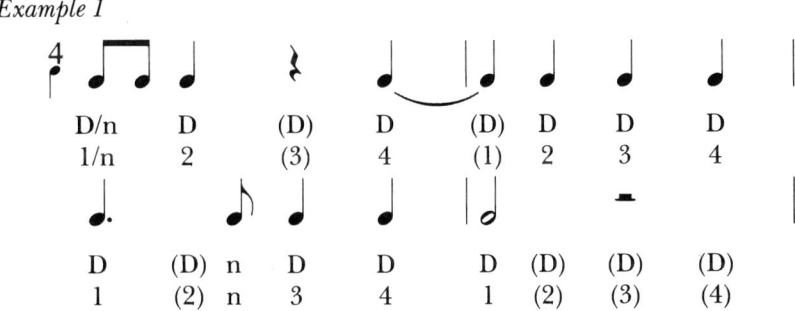

Example 2

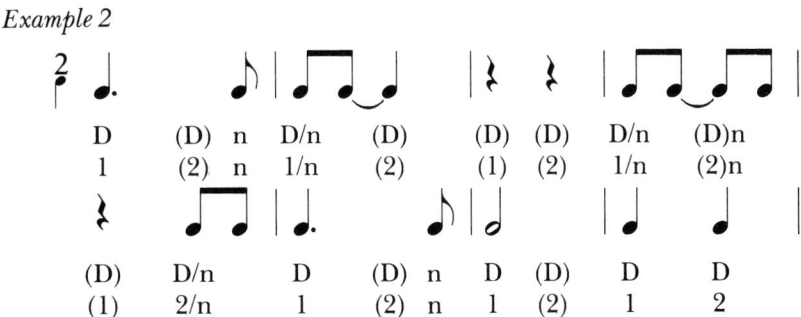

Syncopation

As rhythms use more varied combinations of note values, ties, dots, and rests, what you hear is more interesting, grabbing your attention because it is often a surprise or is unexpected. This happens because of another fundamental device in rhythm: syncopation. The word syncopation comes from the Greek word *syn-ko-pe,* which means to cut short or suspend. It is actually the Greek word for heart attack, a temporary suspension of circulation and breathing. In music it refers to a temporary displacement of the regular stressed and unstressed beat pattern. You have heard and performed examples of syncopation many times in your life. It is a very common aspect of rhythm. It is something we do naturally when we are singing or playing a song. Not every song has syncopation in it, but many folk songs do. The two most common examples of syncopation that you have experienced in this class are shown below. (Notice that the actual syncopations are circled.)

When a rest occurs in an unexpected place in the music, especially on a stressed beat, it results in a sort of surprise—no sound when you expected it. This is one form of syncopation. Look at the songs "Rocka My Soul" (the seventh measure) and "Tom Dooley" (the second and eighth measures). In the example below the rhythm has been altered to make it syncopated. This example is from the song "Michael, Row the Boat Ashore."

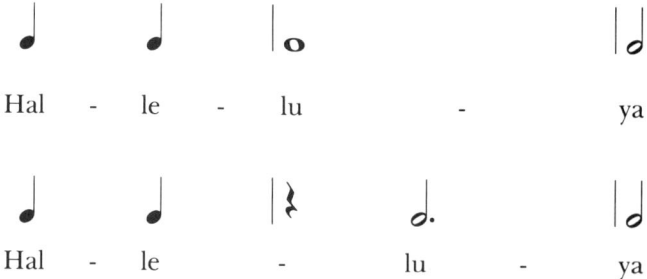

In another example of syncopation, the beginning of a beat (the second) is actually held over from the previous beat, thus upsetting the regularity of the beat feeling. This explanation may sound more confusing than seeing it in notation. In the following examples, a phrase from "Jolly Old Saint Nicholas" has been altered to make it syncopated. The syncopated rhythm should have the same sound as:

SHORT   L O N G   SHORT

Study these examples by speaking the rhythm with Du's, with numbers, and with words.

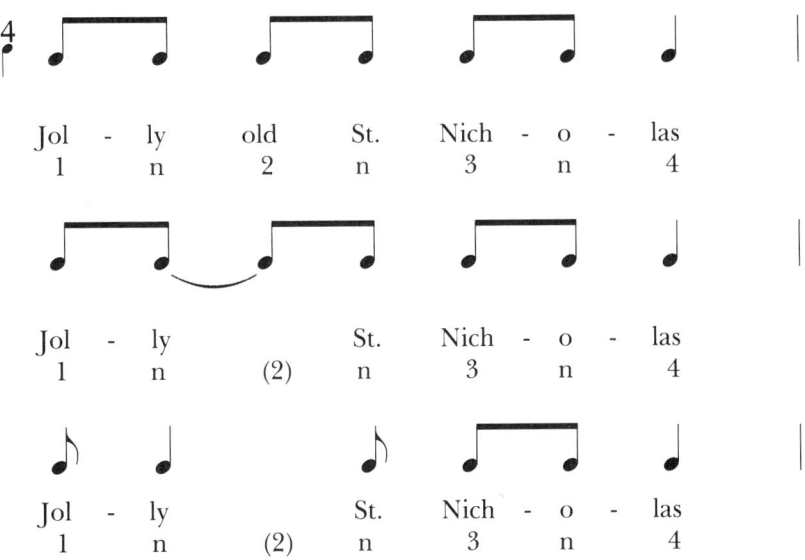

Here is an example of syncopation from the song "Tom Dooley." The first line shows the rhythm *not* syncopated; the second and third lines show the rhythm syncopated and notated two ways.

♪ **Perform** ♪
Songs 7A and 7B on the recorder

Now you are ready to perform songs with syncopation and understand the rhythmic notation. Be sure to study the rhythm of each of these songs before you play them. As you play "Tom Dooley" on the recorder (Songs 7A and 7B), pay particular attention to the rhythm in each version. Notice how predictable and "square" the rhythm of Song 7A is compared to the more interesting, natural rhythm of Song 7B. It is probably much more difficult for you to play the 7A version because it is un-natural and forced. Yet it is important for you to be able to read rhythm correctly, whether it is syncopated or not.

When you perform an accompaniment with a song that has syncopation in it, the beat must be kept steady to provide contrast for the syncopation.

♪ **Perform** ♪
"Sloop John B."
Song 27

What You Have Experienced in This Encounter

Counting the beats in a measure
The G chord on the guitar
Syncopated rhythms

To Further Your Understanding

1. Continue to practice speaking and tapping "The Du Nay Du Cakewalk."
2. When you are ready, practice strumming the chords on "The Du Nay Du Cakewalk" as you count the rhythm.
3. Continue to practice "Sloop John B."
4. Look at Song 28, "Down by the Riverside." How many examples of syncopation can you find? Try to speak the words of the song in the correct rhythms. This may be somewhat difficult in places, but try to see how successful you can be.
5. On a piece of staff paper, copy the notation for the song "Sloop John B." Try to make your notation as neat as possible. You do not need to copy the words.
   a. Write in the counting (numbers) for the melody rhythm.
   b. How many examples of syncopation can you find to circle?
   Note: You may wonder whether the eighth measure is syncopated because of the rest. It is not because the word "Let" is on an important beat in ⁴ meter. You may also wonder about the rhythm in the thirteenth measure. Yes, "so broke up" is syncopated. When you tie a note into a beat, it creates a hesitation on the beat, which is another way of syncopating a rhythm. This may be difficult for you to understand at this point.

MUSICAL ENCOUNTER 12
MORE RHYTHM AND FORM

Introducing

Sixteenth notes
Adding a percussion accompaniment
D.S
Coda

What You Will Need

A tuned guitar and your Songbook

The idea of rhythmically subdividing the steady beat was introduced in an earlier encounter. Each beat was divided exactly in half through the use of eighth notes:

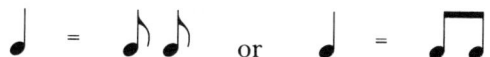

If you think of the beat as a way to measure time, much like a second, minute, hour, or year, it is easy to realize that each beat can be divided into many equal parts, not just in half. One of the most common beat divisions is into four equal parts. You can hear this sound by maintaining a steady beat with your foot and saying the word Mis-sis-sip-pi on each beat. This four-part division is notated with sixteenth notes. A sixteenth note consists of a body, stem, and two flags:

Like eighth notes, sixteenth notes can be written separately or combined. When combined, they have two beams as opposed to eighth notes, which have only one.

Eighth notes   Sixteenth notes

When applying rhythm syllables to sixteenth notes, those already learned are still used (i.e., Du's and nay's). However, "te's" are used between them as shown below. Give this new syllable a very soft, unstressed sound as in "Tibet."

Du   nay   Du   te   nay   te

Eighth notes   Sixteenth notes

It is common to combine sixteenth notes with notes of other rhythmic values. For example, three very popular patterns combine an eighth note with two sixteenth notes. The following three patterns are so common that *you should memorize them* so that when you see them, you will automatically know how they sound.

Du   nay - te   or   Du - te nay   or   Du te (nay) te

"The Du Te Nay Te Rap" in the Songbook will give you some practice with sixteenth notes. As you practice the rap, be sure to do so slowly, making sure that the rhythm and syllables are accurate.

In this rap a section is repeated verbatim. To save notation space, a shorthand designation is used. You will need to understand it before you can perform. If you remember the term D.C. al Fine from an earlier encounter, you will understand how this new designation works. The marking *D.S. al Coda* is an abbreviation for the Italian *Dal Segno al Coda*, meaning "Go back to the 'sign' and continue until you see the coda marking." Thus when you see the term D.S. al Coda, you repeat from the sign until you reach the coda marking, then jump to the section of the music that is called the *coda*, translated in English as "ending."

Sign   Coda marking

♪ **Perform** ♪
"The Du Te Nay Te Rap"

"The Du Te Nay Te Rap" incorporates D.S. al Coda and sixteenth notes. To become comfortable with all of these aspects, you will need to practice the piece many times. When you do practice it, try to maintain its rhythmic accuracy.

Another new aspect of ensemble playing is to have instruments play something that will embellish the beat or rhythm of the melody. These instruments are part of the family of *percussion* instruments, which are sounded by shaking or striking one object against another. Drums, tambourines, maracas, claves, and triangles are examples of percussion instruments. They are most often used to maintain or embellish the beat in an ensemble. If you were merely to maintain the beat in the rap, you would play the following notes on an instrument.

To create a part for a percussion instrument to embellish the beat, either choose certain interesting measures of rhythm from the song or create your own. Here are three examples:

Using these examples as ostinatos, plan an accompaniment for the rap by assigning a percussion instrument to each part. A suggested accompaniment is given here, but you should also try other arrangements of instruments. Certain percussion instruments sound better on certain rhythms. For instance, a triangle would not sound good on a measure of sixteenth notes.

Stressed beat: Triangle

Beat: Drum

Pattern one: Tambourine

Pattern two: Claves

Pattern three: Maracas

♪ **Perform** ♪
"The Du Te Nay Te Rap" with
percussion accompaniment

When you are ready to perform the rap with this accompaniment, it would be wise to stagger instrument and voice entrances so that each part is established before another part begins. Begin with the beat, add the stressed beat, then add each ostinato one at a time, and finally add the speaking voices. Don't forget to add expression to your performance. Good luck!

What You Have Experienced in This Encounter

Sixteenth notes
Adding a percussion accompaniment
D.S
Coda

To Further Your Understanding

1. Add "The Du Te Nay Te Rap" to your rehearsal grid.
2. Below are the rhythm syllables for patterns learned in this encounter. Notate the correct rhythm above each example.

    a. Du te nay   d. Du te nay te

    b. Du   nay   e. Du   nay te

    c. Du te   te   f. Du   te

3. Write in the rhythm syllables for the following phrase of rhythm. Use the Du nay syllables and, below, translate them into counting beats. (1 nay, etc.)

4. (A reverse exercise) Notate the rhythm expressed by the following rhythm syllables.

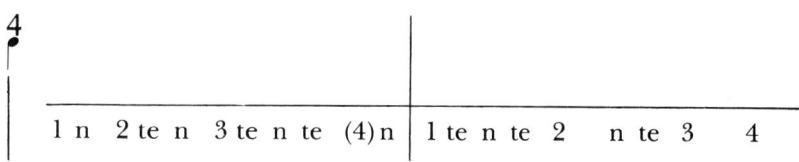

1 n   2 te n   3 te n te   (4) n | 1 te n te   2   n te 3   4

MUSICAL ENCOUNTER 13
MUSICAL EXPRESSION

Introducing

Expression through:

Fermata	Rubato	Decrescendo
Dynamics	Accelerando	a Tempo
Contrasts	Ritard	p
Legato	Tempo markings	f
Staccato	Crescendo	m

What You Will Need

Your Songbook

In the last encounter, "The Du Te Nay Te Rap" introduced you to the sixteenth note, which subdivides a beat into four equal parts. "The Du Te Nay Te Rap" will now introduce you to perhaps the most important and most fundamental aspect of music—expression.

Expression in Music

Music would not hold such a prominent place in society if large numbers of people did not find it to be expressive. All performers try to make their music as expressive as possible to the listener. The energy of rock groups, melancholy of ballad singers, and sincerity of religious singers are all attempts by performers to convey meaning of some sort to their audience. This communication is so important that many musicians feel that expression is the *most important* skill a performer possesses.

Many beginning performers are so concerned with perfecting their new skills or so preoccupied with remembering them that they never think of expression. This is a shame because even the most basic song can be made beautiful by carefully applied expressive techniques.

Many expression techniques are not written by the music composer but instead are left to the taste and creativity of the individual performer. However, some expressive markings are often notated on the music; these markings are discussed in this encounter.

Dynamics

Dynamics simply refer to the volume of sound being produced. Manipulating dynamics is perhaps the most common way for a performer to vary the music to try to convey meaning. For example, the sad verse of a song often is sung softly; a joyous song is performed louder. Three letters (p, f, and m) are used to indicate the volume level of the performance. These letters each represent an Italian word:

Letter	Italian word	English translation
p	Piano	Soft
f	Forte	Loud
m	Mezzo	Half

These three letters can be combined to produce a variety of dynamic levels as follows:

ppp	very, very soft
pp	very soft
p	soft
mp	half soft
mf	half loud
f	loud
ff	very loud
fff	very, very loud

To indicate changes in dynamics, such as a general increase from p to mp or a decrease from f to mf, a crescendo or decrescendo is used. These markings are as follows:

p   *mp*   *f*   *mf*
Crescendo   Descrescendo

As with most expression markings, dynamics can be used at the start of a piece of music to indicate an overall quality or anywhere within a piece to indicate a change.

Tempo Markings

The second most common type of expressive decision that the performer makes is to choose, change, or alter a tempo. To help with this, a *tempo marking* is often at the beginning of a piece of music. The tempo marking consists of a note value, equal sign, and number. The number indicates how many of the designated note values there should be per minute. Thus quarter note = 80 means that there should be about 80 quarter notes per minute. A mechanical or electronic device called a metronome, which produces an audible beat (a clicking sound) at a desired speed, can then be set to mark the appropriate tempo.

Another common way to designate tempo is through the use of Italian terms. Although this is less precise than the metronome marking technique, it is still very common. Eight common terms are used for designating tempo. Arranged from slowest to fastest, these terms and their translations are:

Italian term	*English translation*
Largo	Broad
Lento	Slow
Adagio	Slow, at ease
Andante	Walking
Moderato	Moderate
Allegretto, Allegro	Fast; cheerful
Presto	Very fast
Prestissimo	As fast as possible

Once a tempo has been established, a very expressive technique is to alter that tempo. Since we expect that a tempo will not change throughout a piece (and it usually doesn't), a tempo change can be very exciting. For example, a piece of music that progressively gets faster creates the effect of excitement. Alternately, a piece that slows down often creates a calming effect. To indicate a general acceleration of the tempo, the term *accelerando* (Italian, meaning "becoming faster") is used. This term is easy to remember because of its similarity to the word accelerate; it is literally like stepping on the accelerator of a car to speed it up. The opposite effect of slowing down the tempo is achieved through the use of the term *ritard* (or rit.).

Two other expressive markings that alter the steady beat are common and useful to you as a performer: a rubato and a fermata. A *rubato* is used for short sections of a piece of music where an elastic (or flexible) tempo is desired. Throughout a section marked with a rubato, the performer is free to play faster or slower, according to the requirements of the musical expression. To end a rubato section, the term *a tempo*, meaning "back to the normal tempo," is used.

A *fermata* instructs the performer to literally stop the beat at a certain point, holding whatever note is being performed. This marking appears as: ⌒ The pitch under the fermata is "held" for the length of time that a performer feels is appropriate.

Finally, two expressive markings reflect the manner in which the actual pitches are to be performed. Sometimes the pitches sound more expressive if they are performed smoothly, almost as if they were connected. In this case the music is marked *legato*. The opposite of legato, where each pitch is distinctly separated from the previous one, is designated by the word *staccato* or by putting a dot (like a period) under each note as shown below.

It is important to note that all of these expressive markings are used to add variety, contrast, and interest to your performance. Even if they are not marked in the music, it is your right as a performer to use any and all of these techniques wherever you feel it is appropriate. They can be especially important when a section of the music is repeated.

One final note: Many students who are studying music notation for the first time question why markings such as those discussed in this encounter need to be in Italian. It would seem that learning notation is confusing enough without having to learn Italian words as well! There is actually a practical reason for using these terms. The Italian designations are accepted around the world as the standard. Therefore a composer in Russia, France, Germany, Brazil, or the United States will designate their expression markings in Italian. Imagine the confusion if composers used their native languages simply to designate that they wanted a piece played "as fast as possible." In the long run, learning the accepted terminology saves much time and frustration.

Try "The Du Te Nay Te Rap" again, paying particular attention to making it expressive. As the famous conductor Leonard Bernstein put it so beautifully: "Damn the mistakes. Full speed ahead!"

♪ **Perform** *p*
"The Du Te Nay Te Rap"

What You Have Experienced in This Encounter

Expression through:

Dynamics	Decrescendo	Fermata
p	Tempo markings	a Tempo
f	Accelerando	Legato
m	Ritard	Staccato
Crescendo	Rubato	Contrasts

To Further Your Understanding

1. Add "The Du Te Nay Te Rap" with expression to your rehearsal grid.
2. Add some expressive techniques to at least two other songs that you are practicing.
3. Explain in a few words, the meaning of the following musical symbols and terms.

a. ⌢ꞏ

h. ◁

b. *mf*

i. accelerando

c. adagio

j. pianissimo

d. dynamics

k. cresc.

e. forte

l. rit.

f. andante

m. allegretto

g. legato

n. ♩ꞏ

4. Try this for practice. Read the alphabet below, following the musical signs. Some symbols and terms are already there, but you are to add six more that you learned in this encounter and in Encounter 12. Practice reciting the alphabet as you follow the signs. Give your copy to another class member, and see how well they perform your "arrangement" of the alphabet.

𝄋

A   B   C   D   E   F   G   H   I   J   K   L   M

f

D. S.

‖: N   O   P   Q   R   S   :‖ T   U   V   W   X   Y   Z

rit.

MUSICAL ENCOUNTER 14
APPLYING THE MAJOR SCALE: FINDING THE STARTING PITCH OF A SONG

Introducing

The G major chord (review)
Do-Mi-Sol of the scale
Finding the key of a song

What You Will Need

Your Songbook
A recorder
A guitar

This Encounter reviews the G major chord with a new song. The G major chord is one of the more difficult chords you will learn and therefore you may still be having trouble with it. The following suggestions should help.

Figure 14-1

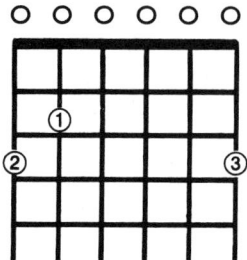 or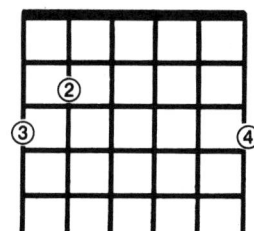

G major chord

Finger the chord and strum all six strings as indicated in Figure 14-1. If you are having difficulty getting all the strings to sound clearly, pick each string individually while you are holding the chord. Adjust the placement of each finger until every string "sings." With practice, you will make these adjustments automatically.

When this chord is combined with the chords learned earlier (D, A7, and E minor), many songs can be played. This is because all of these chords are related to the scale of D major. Therefore it is almost as if these chords are from the same family. This phenomenon will be explored in more detail later. Suffice it to say that it is important to be able to move fluently between all of the chords learned this far. To develop this desired fluidity, play the following progression as part of your daily practice period.

Exercise in the Scale of D Major

Play one measure (4 beats) of each of the following chords. Be sure to play it slow enough to maintain a steady beat, even during changes.

$$\frac{4}{} \;\|: \quad D \;|\; G \;|\; D \;|\; A7 \;|\; D \;|\; G \;|\; Em \;|\; A7 \;|\; D \;:\|$$

♪ Perform ♪
"Michael, Row the Boat Ashore"
Song 11

You have already played Song 11, "Michael, Row the Boat Ashore" on the recorder. Now that you know the G major chord, you can play it on the guitar as well. This song would sound good as an ensemble. Be sure to strive for a proper balance of volume between recorder, voice, and guitar.

Now try to play the first three pitches of the melody on your recorder as notated below. These three pitches, Do-Mi-Sol, are the most important pitches for determining what scale is being used in a song. Most songs are written using only the notes of one specific scale. Song 11 is written using the D major scale—only pitches from that scale will be found anywhere in the song.

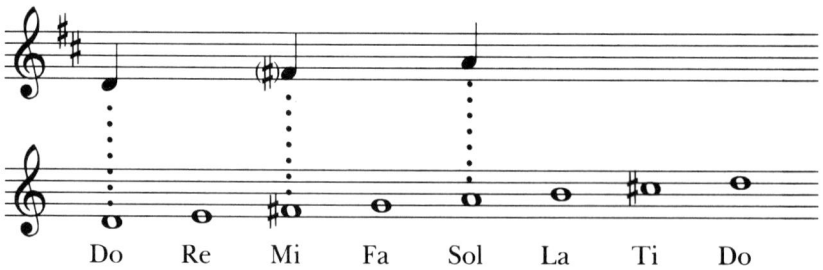

Notice that these three pitches correspond to Do-Mi-Sol in the D major scale notated here.

Key

In most songs you will find that only the seven pitch names of a specific scale are used. Of course, these seven pitches can be repeated many times. They can also be arranged in an almost endless variety of patterns, according to the composer's wishes. Still, most of the pitches in a given song are from a particular scale. When referring to the scale used for a specific song, we use the term *key*. Thus a song written with the pitches from the D major scale is said to be in the key of D major; the G scale denotes the key of G major; and so forth.

Of the seven possible pitches in a scale, Do-Mi-Sol are the most important to a singer or song leader because almost all songs will begin on either Do, Mi, or Sol of the scale in which the song is written. Therefore a good skill to have is the ability to find and sing Do-Mi-Sol in the key of the song.

The pitches Do-Mi-Sol should be sung at the start of every song to develop this ability. For practice, try strumming the first chord of Song 11 on your guitar while *singing* the first three notes of the song, Do-Mi-Sol. After singing these notes for a while, it will become as automatic as riding a bike.

One suggestion for practicing this skill is to sing the pitches of Do-Mi-Sol in an interesting rhythm. Play the melody notated below on the recorder. Then play the harmony on the guitar while singing the pitches of the pattern.

You can also sing the final pitch Sol one octave lower. Although this cannot be played on the recorder, you should practice singing it in this manner. Many songs begin on the Sol, which is below Do.

These exercises can be sung at any pitch level, according to the key in which a song is written. You will learn to move pitches to other keys (called transposing) in Encounter 15.

Finding Do

The pitches Do-Mi-Sol can be sung in any key. The key you choose depends on the key in which a song is written. Look at the last chord of the song to find the appropriate key. This chord usually has the same name as the key of the song. Strum this chord to see if you can hear the pitch of Do (Do-Mi-Sol are all present in this chord). If you cannot discern which pitch is Do, then pluck whichever string on the guitar is the lowest string played for that chord. This is the single pitch of Do. If you still are having trouble finding Do, play the pitch on the recorder that corresponds with the chord name. For example, if you find a song with a final chord of G major, Do is the pitch G. Likewise, if you have a song ending on an E♭ chord, the pitch of E♭ is Do for that song.

If the song does not have chord symbols above the melody, you could try playing the last melody pitch of the song. This pitch is *often* Do. Unfortunately, this method for finding the key is not as certain as the chord method.

Finding the Starting Singing Pitch

Once you can easily sing Do, followed by Mi-Sol, the next step to find the starting singing pitch of a song is to determine whether the song begins on Do, Mi, or Sol. Look at the first pitch of the song. In the scale of the song, determine whether that pitch is Do, Mi, or Sol. (Occasionally it will *not* be one of these.) Sing Do-Mi-Sol again, but this time stop on the appropriate pitch. This is the starting singing pitch.

For practice, look again at Song 11 and follow these steps:

1. Find the last chord. This is the key of the song. It informs you of the name of the scale used in this song.
2. Play the last chord and sing Do-Mi-Sol.
3. Determine whether the song begins on Do, Mi, or Sol. Check your answer with that given in "Introducing Song 11" in your Songbook.
4. Sing Do-Mi-Sol again. This time stop on the starting pitch of the song. Notice how it physically *feels* in your vocal cords to sing this pitch. Remember the pitch and be sure to start singing the song there.

What You Have Experienced in This Encounter

The G major chord
Song 11
Finding the scale of a song
Finding the key of a song
Singing Do-Mi-Sol
Finding the starting pitch of a song

To Further Your Understanding

1. Practice Song 11.
2. Practice singing Do-Mi-Sol.
3. This exercise is designed to give you practice in determining the starting pitch of a song. After you answer the questions, use the guitar or Autoharp to try to find the beginning pitch in your singing voice.

   The following staffs provide the beginning pitch and the final chord of a song. Use the procedure for finding the starting singing pitch as given at the end of this encounter. For each example, name the key, notate Do-Mi-Sol, then circle and name the beginning syllable.

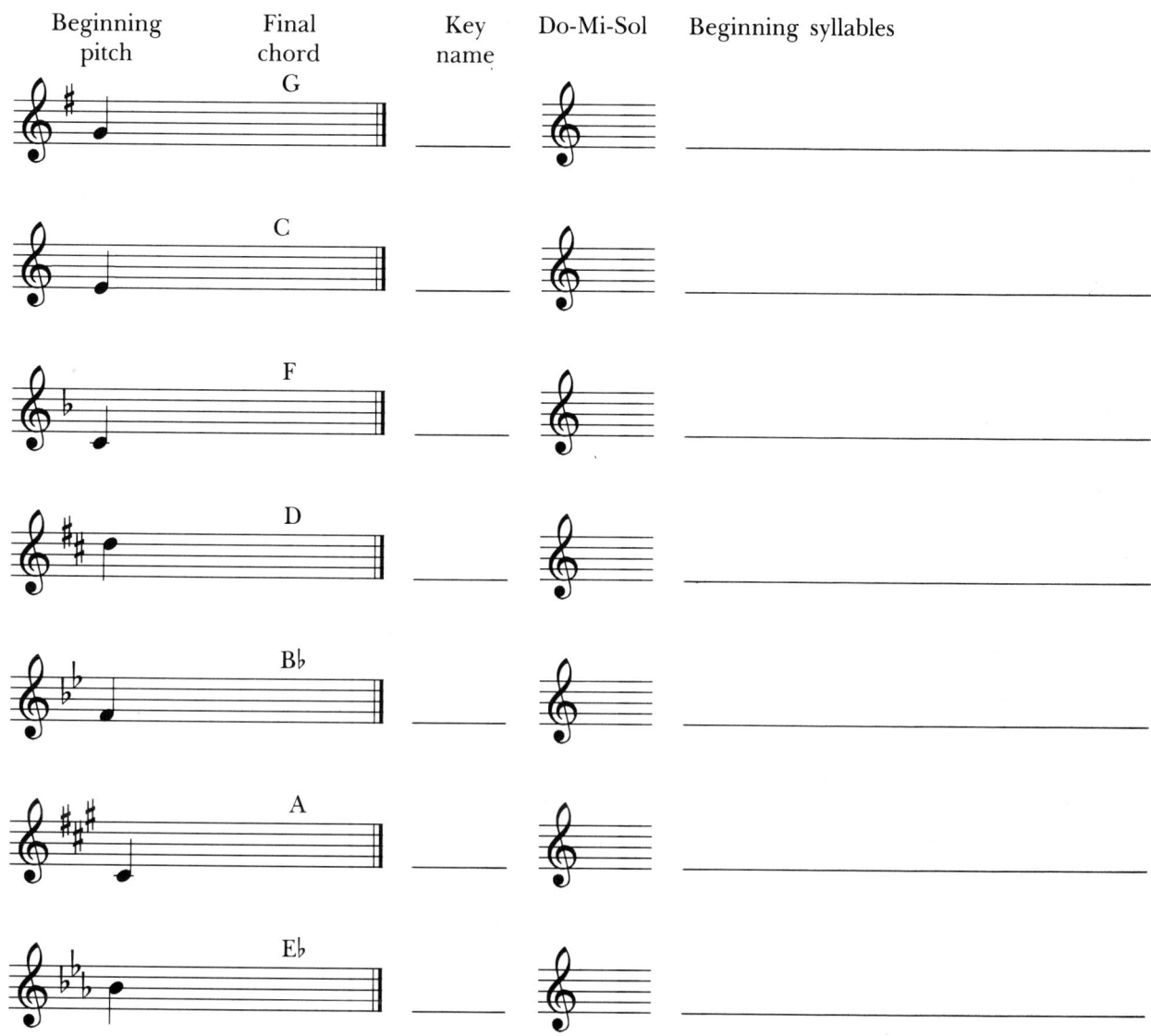

MUSICAL ENCOUNTER 15
APPLYING THE MAJOR SCALE: TRANSPOSING A SONG FROM ONE KEY TO ANOTHER

Introducing

Transposing chords
Chord root
Roman numeral chord symbols

What You Will Need

A tuned guitar and Autoharp

Encounter 10 introduced how to find the specific pitches in a given scale. Encounter 14 discussed how to apply scales to find a starting singing pitch. This encounter leads to one of the more practical uses of scales, namely *transposition*.

As discussed in Encounter 14, when a scale is constructed for a given song, the key of the song is actually being determined. When a song is in the key of G Major, for example, it is primarily composed of the pitches in the G major scale. If the song is in the key of D Major, you can be fairly certain that most of the pitches in that song will be one of the seven pitches in that scale, as shown in the following example.

The pitches of the key of D Major

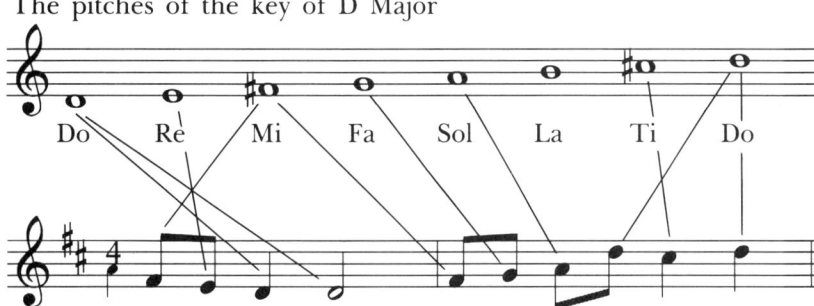

A melody in the key of D Major

The basic *chords* for the key of D Major can be determined in the same way, because each of the pitches becomes the *root* for a chord in the key of D Major. Besides the chord root, two or more other pitches, usually all from the same scale, are combined with the root to complete the chord formation. This encounter focuses only on the root pitch of the chord, because this pitch gives the chord its name. Since the root defines the name of the chord, it follows that a D chord occurs in the key of D, but an A♭ chord does not because there is no A♭ in the scale.

Pitches in a scale are designated with the names Do, Re, Mi, Fa, Sol, La, and Ti. To distinguish pitches from chords, Roman numerals are used. Thus the chords of D Major are designated as follows:

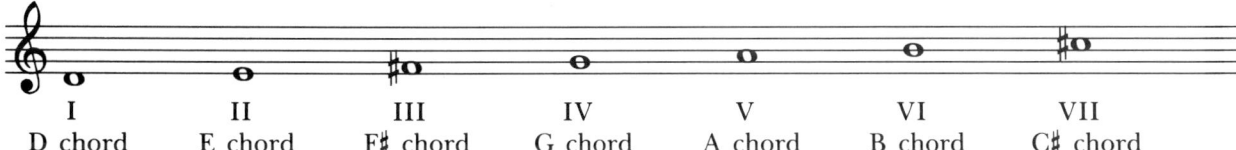

I	II	III	IV	V	VI	VII
D chord	E chord	F♯ chord	G chord	A chord	B chord	C♯ chord

If you are not familiar with Roman numerals, spend a few moments learning the seven numerals in this figure; these are the only ones used in music.

If you were to play the I chord in D Major, you would play the D major chord. What chord would you play as the V chord? If you answered "A," you are right and ready to continue.

The I and the V chord often are considered the fundamental harmony structure of all Western music. Look at Songs 1 through 5 in the Songbook. You will find that each one is composed of only the I and V chord in the key of D Major.

What if one of the songs you performed in this book was too high or too low for you or a group to sing? Finding the I and V chord in a different key would have enabled you to play the song at a different pitch level, either higher or lower. This method of changing the pitch level of a piece of music is called transposition. This word is similar in meaning to the word "transport" in that you will move an *intact* pattern of pitches from one key to another.

Follow the steps provided here to transpose the chords for any song. As an example, you will transpose Song 3, "He's Got the Whole World in His Hands," from the key of D Major (in which it is written) to the key of G Major.

Step 1: Determine the scale of the song before transposition. Notate the scale.

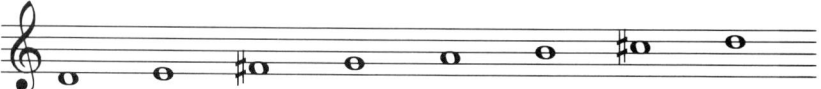

Step 2: Write the Roman numerals for the chords under each pitch.

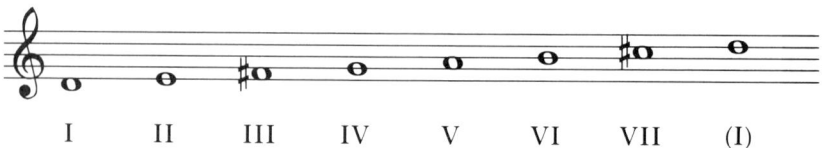

I   II   III   IV   V   VI   VII   (I)

Step 3: Look at the music for the song. Above each chord, puts its Roman numeral equivalent, which you can find from Step 2. For example, the opening chord of Song 3 should look like this:

I
D

Step 4: Construct the scale of the key to which you will transpose. In this case the key is G Major.

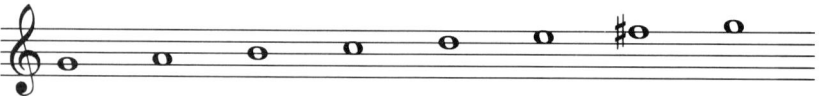

Step 5: Write the Roman numerals for the chords under each pitch of this scale as you did in Step 2.

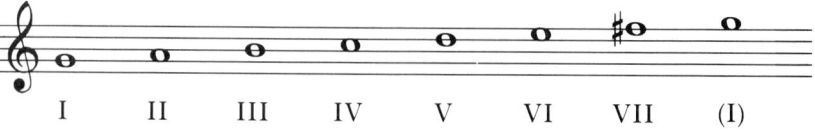

I   II   III   IV   V   VI   VII   (I)

Step 6: Put the new key chord equivalent on the music, above each Roman numeral. For example, the opening chord of "He's Got the Whole World in His Hands" should look like this:

New key --->   G

               I

          D <--Old key

Step 7: If any Arabic numbers, letters, or words appear after the chord name, add these to the transposed chord. For example, if the original chord was A7, then the transposed chord will also have a "7" after it (D7). IF the words "minor" or "suspended" are written after the original chord, then the transposed chord would also have these words. This is also true of letters such as "M," "m," and "sus." *The only designations not brought to the transposed chords are accidentals such as sharps and flats.*

Once you complete the transposition, the song can be performed in either D Major or G Major, depending on which chords are played. Try playing it in both keys. Which is easier to sing? Which do you think would be easier for your class to sing? The difference you note when you sing a song in the two keys is a result of shifting (transposing) the whole pitch pattern higher or lower.

Transposing music works because the relationships between the pitches and chords remain the same when moving from one key to another. Regardless of the pitch in the pitch alphabet on which you begin, the song always sounds like the same song. As long as the relationships between the pitches remain the same, you will recognize the song.

A common song, such as "Happy Birthday to You" which is sung by numerous groups in various voice ranges, may simply be notated using Roman numerals so that it can easily be played in a key appropriate for the voice range of the singers. Then, regardless of whether the song is sung by elementary children or senior citizens, the appropriate pitch can be played.

Try accompanying yourself on guitar while you sing "Happy Birthday" in the key of G. (*Note*: The song begins on low Sol.) This may be an uncomfortable range for you, but it is just right for young children. For adults, simply pick another key and play the appropriate chords. For example, try accompanying the song on the guitar in the key of A or on the Autoharp in the key of F or C.

"Happy Birthday to You"

V7   I   V7
Happy birthday to you,

                        I
Happy birthday to you,

                           IV
Happy birthday, dear Cracktall,

             I   V7 I
Happy birthday to you!

The Roman numeral method is especially useful with an instrument such as the Autoharp, which is designed to transpose easily.

If you look at the buttons of the Autoharp, you will see they are arranged so that the I, IV, and V7 chords in certain keys are within easy reach of each other. This convenient arrangement makes it easy to play songs using the I, IV, and V7 chords in certain keys. For example, play "Happy Birthday" in the keys of C, F, and G. You will find this to be much easier on the Autoharp than on the guitar.

What You Have Experienced in This Encounter

Transposition
Chord root
Roman numeral chord symbols

To Further Your Understanding

1. Pick a song from Part One of the Songbook that was hard for you to sing. Transpose it to another key, play it on either the Autoharp or guitar, and see if it is easier to sing.
2. Transpose the Do-Mi-Sol example on p. 79 to two additional keys.
3. Continue to practice Song 11.
4. Complete the following statements:

    a. The method for changing the pitch level of a piece of music is

       called _____ .

    b. In the key of C, the C chord is called the I chord because _____

       _____

    c. The two most important chords in a key are the I and _____ chord.

5. Transpose the song "Sloop John B." (Song 27) to the key of G, following the steps in this encounter. When you finish, play and sing the song in the new key to see if all the chords sound right. Which key is more comfortable for performing this song?

6. Transpose "Amazing Grace" (Song 26) to the key of F, then sing and accompany yourself on the Autoharp. Be careful on the second line—see whether it is possible to use the alternate chord in parentheses when using the Autoharp.

MUSICAL ENCOUNTER 16
APPLYING THE MAJOR SCALE:
READING THE KEY SIGNATURE

Introducing

Key signatures
Naming the key from the key signature

What You Will Need

A tuned guitar
Your Songbook

When you first look at a song, the scale being used is not immediately apparent. As discussed in the previous encounter, you must first identify the key of a song to determine the scale. In an earlier encounter you were instructed simply to look at the last chord or, in some cases, the last pitch of a song to determine its key. Although this method is easy, it has some unfortunate shortcomings.

First, the last chord method is not foolproof. Sometimes songs end with a chord other than the I chord, although this is unusual. Even more common is a song that ends on a pitch other than Do. This makes the method unusable in some situations. Another, and perhaps more significant, disadvantage of the last chord method is that even if the method does work and the name of the key is found, the scale in use must still be constructed to find the necessary accidentals. For example, by looking at the last chord of Song 10, it can be determined that the song is in the key of D. However, this bit of knowledge does *not* inform you that the pitches of the D scale are D, E, F♯, G, A, B, C♯, D. This means that all pitches of F and C need to be sharped in the song. To find these pitches, you would first have to construct the scale of the song, using the whole-whole-half method described in Encounter 10. This would be awkward and time-consuming to say the least.

Fortunately, there is an easier way. At the beginning of every line of music is a clef and next to it a *key signature*. Key signatures are a fixed order of sharps or flats (including one which has *no* sharps or flats) that identify both the keys of the songs *and* the accidentals to be performed in the appropriate scales. Just as your signature identifies you, a key signature identifies a key.

There are fifteen possible key signatures. Seven identify sharps, seven identify flats, and one identifies no accidentals. Sharps and flats are never mixed in a key signature. Each signature identifies one major and one minor key (minor keys are discussed in a subsequent encounter). Following is a diagram of the key signatures that use sharps.

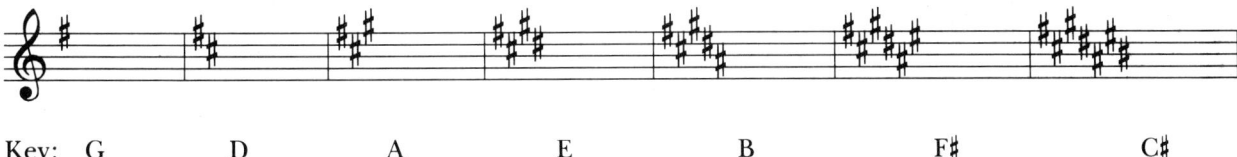

Key: G   D   A   E   B   F♯   C♯

Look at the key signature for D Major with two sharps. This informs you that *all* F and C pitches are sharped in the scale. Notice that for every key, one new sharp is added. Also, all the keys have the sharps in the same order. An easy way to remember the order of sharps is by noting the first letter of each word in this mnemonic sentence:

Frank **C**an't **G**o **D**own **A**nd **E**at **B**ananas = F C G D A E B

Key signatures that identify flats follow a set order in the same way. For each key below, one more flat is added without changing the order of the other flats. From this example, you can see that if you were playing in the key of E♭, all B, E, and A pitches would be flatted.

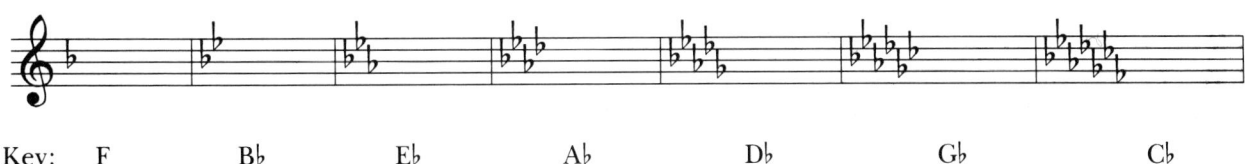

Key: F   B♭   E♭   A♭   D♭   G♭   C♭

The flats are arranged in a standardized order just as are the sharps. To remember the order of flats, simply reverse the order of pitches for sharps, or remember this mnemonic sentence:

Bill **E**ats **A** **D**arn **G**ood **C**at **F**ish = B E A D G C F

As mentioned earlier, one key signature has neither sharps nor flats. This is the key of C Major. When you "see" this key signature depicted, it means that none of the pitches are sharped or flatted. *Remember, a key signature never contains both sharps and flats!*

C Major key signature

Key signatures efficiently and easily inform you of the accidentals present in a given key. This is their main function. However, it is also easy to derive the name of the key from the key signature. Two rules and two exceptions will enable you to do this. Learn the rules and memorize the exceptions.

Rule 1: If the key signature has sharps in it, find the name of the last sharp on the key signature (the one at the right) and go up one-half step on the pitch alphabet. This is the name of the key. For example, the last sharp below is G♯. Go up one-half step from G♯ to the pitch A. The name of the key with three sharps is A Major.

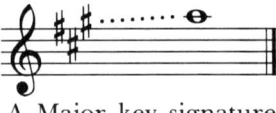

A Major key signature

Rule 2: If the key signature has flats in it, simply look at the name of the second to the last flat; this is the name of the key. In the example below, the second to last flat is E♭; this is the key signature for E♭ Major.

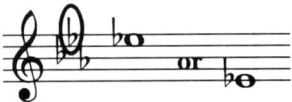

E♭ Major key signature

Exception 1: If there is only one flat in the key signature, it is clearly impossible to find the second to last flat. Rule 2 cannot work in this instance. If there is only one flat, then the key is F Major.

Exception 2: If there are *no* sharps or flats in the key signature, neither rule will work. In this case the key is C Major.

F Major   C Major (No sharps or flats)

You will quickly become accustomed and familiar with key signatures. Just like accomplished musicians, you will soon automatically look at the key signature before playing the first pitch of the song. You will also get used to seeing some of the more popular key signatures and will probably recognize these on sight. Even if you are not interested in knowing the name of the key, it is still critical that you look at the key signature to determine if any accidentals are needed to perform the song.

Following are some additional points to ponder.

1. There are only fifteen key signatures, and they always denote the same keys. When you see a key signature of three flats, it will always look the same and signify the same major key. The three flats will always be the same three flats in the same order as shown:

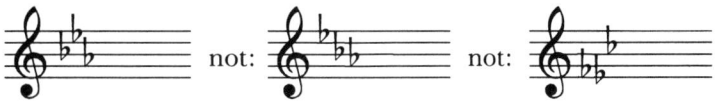

2. Another way to identify flat keys is to remember that the last flat is always the fourth degree (Fa) of the scale. Thus you can name a key by moving down two and one-half steps from the last flat to find Do. This point eliminates the need for *Exception 1* previously noted.

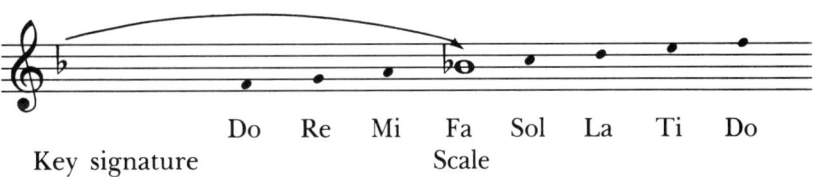

Key signature   Do   Re   Mi   Fa   Sol   La   Ti   Do
                                              Scale

What You Have Experienced in This Encounter

Determining the accidentals to be played from the key signature
Identifying the name of the key from the key signature

To Further Your Understanding

1. Continue to practice the songs on your rehearsal grid.
2. For each of the following musical examples, answer the questions by completing the statements.

A. The key signature for this song is _____.
B. The song is in the key of _____.
C. The scale for the song will be _____.
D. The key note (or Do) is _____.
E. Do-Mi-Sol in this key is _____.

A. The key signature for this song is _____.
B. The song is in the key of _____.
C. The scale for the song will be _____.
D. The key note (or Do) is _____.
E. Do-Mi-Sol in this key is _____.

A. The key signature for this song is _____.
B. The song is in the key of _____.
C. The scale for the song will be _____.
D. The key note (or Do) is _____.
E. Do-Mi-Sol in this key is _____.

MUSICAL ENCOUNTER 17
APPLYING THE MAJOR SCALE: CREATING AN INTRODUCTION TO A SONG

Introducing

Introductions
C natural (♮) on the recorder
A minor (Am), C Major on the guitar
Pick-up notes
Church lick strum

What You Will Need

Your Songbook
A recorder
A guitar

Almost every song you hear on the radio has a short musical beginning before the melody. These "beginnings" are called *introductions* and they perform several important functions for the singer.

An introduction provides the singer with aural (sound) information about the key in which the song is being performed. During the introduction, the singer (or singers) listens carefully to find the starting pitch. It is easier to find the pitch this way than by simply hearing a single pitch played on the guitar, recorder, or piano. A secure introduction, combined with establishing a good beginning pitch, therefore results in improved and more confident group singing.

A good introduction provides the singer (and listener) with two additional performance clues. First, the tempo is inherent in the introduction of the song, enabling a group of singers to begin together without a count-off. The other clue provided by an introduction is the mood of the song, which prepares the singer to perform happily, energetically, sadly, or in whatever manner that words alone cannot express.

It is really quite easy to compose an introduction to a song. The first step is to establish the length of the introduction. Most introductions you have heard are either two or four measures in length. A four-measure introduction is preferred for amateur singers in that it provides twice as much time for the singer to prepare to sing. For this reason, you should try to compose four-measure introductions.

The second step is to determine the chords to play. Since a primary purpose of the introduction is to establish the key of the song, it makes sense that the first chord should be the I chord. Hearing this chord will firmly establish the key for the singers and the audience. For the song "Yankee Doodle," your introduction will start like this:

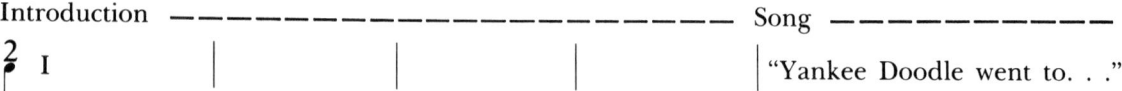

The second most important chord in any key is the V7 chord. As discussed in Encounter 15, many songs are written with only the I and V7 chords. The reason this is possible is that the V7 chord in any key has a pulling tendency to the I chord. Try playing the I chord, followed by the V7 chord, in any key. You will probably notice a pulling tendency back to the I chord. Playing the I chord will make the progression sound complete. The song leader can use this natural tendency to good advantage and encourage a group to sing. Since most songs begin with the I chord, an introduction that ends on the V7 chord will "pull" the singers into the song. Thus they will sing with more confidence than with an introduction ending in any other chord. This introduction is as shown below.

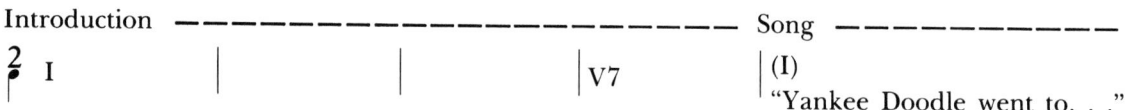

Because the I and V7 chords are so fundamental to music, they provide a very strong support structure for this introduction. These two chords can be described as the "bookends" for the chords occurring in the middle. They are so powerful that it does not much matter which two chords fill the middle two measures. The only rule is that the two middle chords should be from the same key as the I and V7 chords. A good way to determine them is to look through the song, pick two more chords from the song, and play them to decide which sound the best. Ultimately, your ear will be your guide.

Following is one introduction possibility. Play it in the key of D Major.

Introduction ——————————————————— Song ——————————

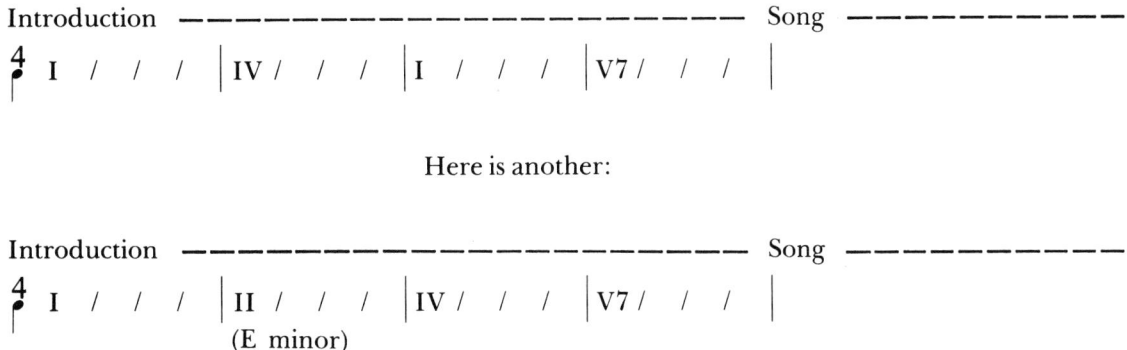

Here is another:

Although they are different, either introduction would work in a song. Settle on one by asking, "Which introduction best suits the song?" and, more importantly, "Which one do I like?"

One fundamental consideration to remember when creating introductions (or any part of music) is that although concrete rules exist for writing music (in this case an introduction), music that follows every rule would all sound similar and quite boring. Beauty often results from *breaking* the rules. Therefore, use the suggestions provided here as guidelines, but let your ear and common musical sense be your ultimate guide.

To ensure that your group will sing well, you can also count off during the final measure of the introduction. Try reciting the words "ready sing" on the two beats preceding the starting note of the song. Thus, depending on the meter signature, you could use one of the following:

3 beats: "1- ready sing"
2 beats: "ready sing"

Introduction ——————————————————— Song ——————————

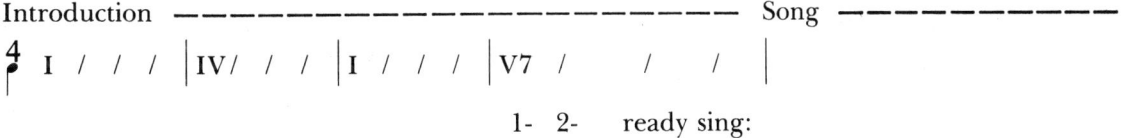

1- 2-   ready sing:

It is also beneficial if you *sing* the count-off on the starting pitch of the song. Try putting the above introduction on "Rocka My Soul" (Song 4). Sing the count-off on an F♯ while playing.

Pick-Up Notes

The rules for writing an introduction must be slightly modified for songs that use what is known as a *pick-up note*, or anacrusis. A pick-up note (or notes) is placed before the first *full* measure of the song; it is performed during the last measure of the introduction and serves a very useful function.

To understand this function, you must recall the discussion in Encounter 4 of the steady beat being divided into units of stressed and unstressed beats. It was established that the first beat of a measure is the one that will usually get the stress. When composers write songs, however, they are often confronted with a situation in which the first word of the text is not an accented word, such as the following examples:

"There **was** a farmer **had** a dog and **Bing**o was his **name**-o"
or
"When **John**ny comes marching **home** again"

In these examples, the words "Johnny" and "was" are accented, but not the words "when" or "there." Try to sing with an accent on the word "when" or "there," and you will find how unnatural this feels.

To place the accent where it belongs, both in the measure and on the words, the composer simply "picked up" the unaccented word and moved it into the introduction. This then allowed the naturally accented word to be placed on the first beat of the first full measure of the song. The note that is moved into the introduction is called a pick-up note.

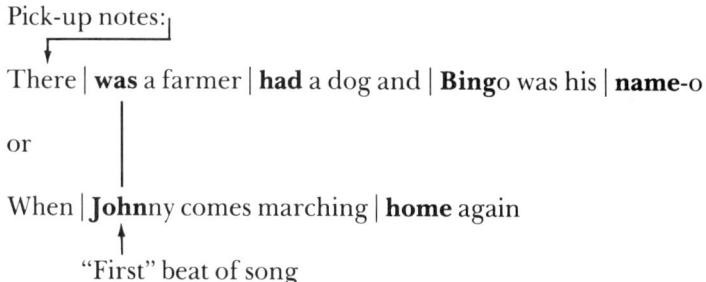

Pick-up notes:

There | **was** a farmer | **had** a dog and | **Bing**o was his | **name**-o

or

When | **John**ny comes marching | **home** again

"First" beat of song

Any number of pick-up notes may be placed at the start of a song. For example, speak the phrases below, keeping the stress on the word "cats." Also practice counting off the phrase as written.

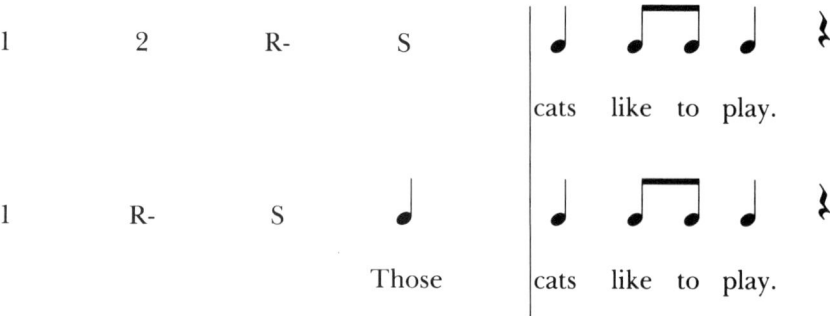

1   2   R-   S   cats like to play.

1   R-   S   ♩   Those   cats like to play.

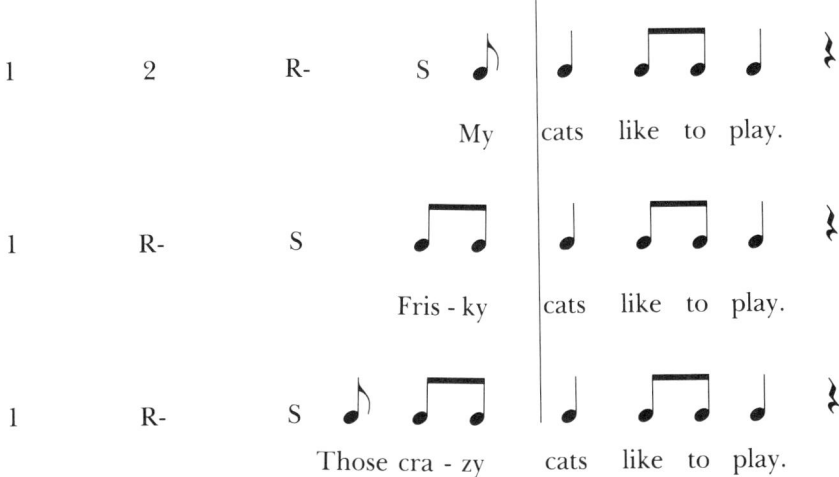

| 1 | 2 | R- | S | | My | cats | like | to | play. |

| 1 | R- | S | | Fris - ky | cats | like | to | play. |

| 1 | R- | S | | Those cra - zy | cats | like | to | play. |

Obviously, when a song begins with a pick-up note, it is necessary to modify the introduction to account for it. The pick-up note(s) becomes part of the last measure of your introduction as shown here:

Introduction   Song

1- ready sing: "The   bug

Both Songs 13 and 14 start with a pick-up note. However, before they can be performed the A *minor* chord must be learned on the guitar and the C♮, which is pronounced "C natural" and is different from the C♯ learned previously, must be learned on the recorder.

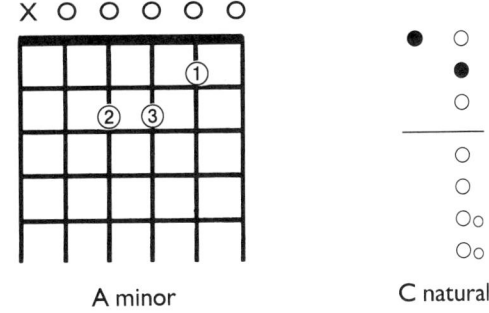

A minor   C natural

♪ **Perform** ƒ
"Simple Gifts"
Song 13

You are now ready to play Song 13 in the Songbook. Practice the recorder part, then the guitar part. Later it can be performed as a class ensemble with some students playing guitar, others playing recorders. Use the introduction on page 97 or make up your own. Rehearse, emphasizing proper balance, mood, tempo, and, of course, no mistakes.

♪ **Perform** ƒ
"It's a Small World"
Song 14

You are also ready to begin work on Song 14. However, the entire song cannot be played on the recorder. Therefore, practice only the chorus on the recorder and the entire song on the guitar.

Both of these songs would be greatly enhanced using a different strum than what you have learned so far. This seems like an appropriate place to introduce the strum called the *church lick*, because it works so well with Songs 13 and 14 and will also prepare you for the next encounter.

The Church Lick

In earlier encounters you used the eighth note to subdivide the beat in half:

Du nay Du nay Du nay Du nay

You also divided it again using sixteenth notes:

Du te nay te Du te nay te Du te nay te Du te nay te

These subdivisions are referred to as duple because they divide the beat in half or multiples of halves. If you use a strum that displays this subdivision, the accompaniment will sound more energized and interesting. This is the principle behind the church lick strum.

The *unstressed* beats in the church lick are subdivided with eighth notes:

This subdivided pattern is accomplished by flicking the index finger in a down-up pattern in the eighth-note rhythm.

Rhythm:
Strum
direction:

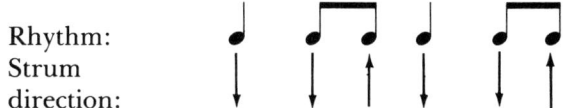

To achieve speed, the down stroke should only strike the top three strings; the up stroke should only strike one or two strings. The quarter note is played with a down stroke on the lowest strings of the chord.

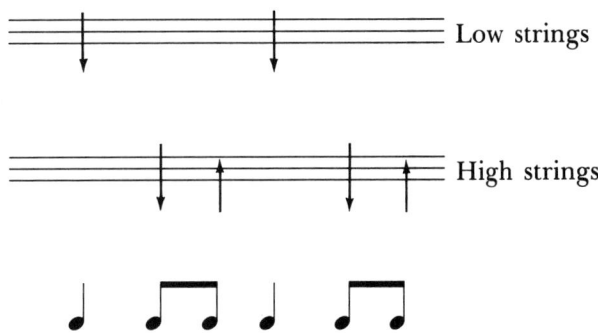

Low strings

High strings

Practice the church lick on one chord until you are comfortable with it. Then try a progression that changes chords. Only after it feels like second nature are you ready to try it in a song.

What You Have Experienced in This Encounter

Introductions
Pick-up notes
A minor (Am), C Major on the guitar
C natural on the recorder
Songs 13 and 14
Church lick strum

To Further Your Understanding

1. Add Songs 13 and 14 to both your recorder and guitar practice grid.
2. Compose introductions for Songs 12 through 14.
3. Here are the beginnings of four songs. Plan an appropriate introduction for each song. Pay particular attention to the key signature and meter signature. Write out a four-measure introduction for guitar or Autoharp, and write in the count-off for the singers.

MUSICAL ENCOUNTER 18
TRIPLE DIVISION OF THE BEAT

Introducing

The E7 and D7 guitar chords
Triple feeling of the beat
The Du nah nee sound
High E on the recorder

What You Will Need

A guitar
A recorder

Using the diagram of the E7 chord, find the chord on the guitar and practice it in the following progression.

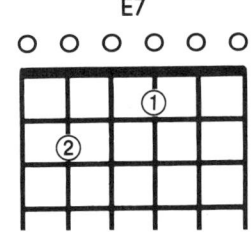

2 D | D | E7 | E7 | A7 | A7 | D | D ‖

If you pay close attention to the movement of your first finger, you will notice that it does not move very far from one chord to the other. As soon as you are comfortable playing this progression of chords, you are ready to play and sing a familiar song.

♪ **Perform** ♪
"Over The River"
Song 12

Once you have performed this old favorite, listen and concentrate on the rhythm of the words as it relates to the beat. As you say the words aloud in rhythm, snap your fingers and sway from side to side on the beat. Notice where the natural stressed beats fall:

"Ov . . . . riv . . . . through . . . . woods"

Also notice how each beat is divided into thirds. This division of the beat is called *triple*.

Repeat the following phrases over and over until you are sure you feel and hear the triple division of the beat. Continue to sway from side to side and snap your fingers on the beat.

"O - ver - the RI - ver and,"   ⟩ . .   ⟩ . .

"GRAND-fa - ther, GRAND-fa - ther"   ⟩ . .   ⟩ . .

Now go back and substitute these rhythm syllables for the above words.

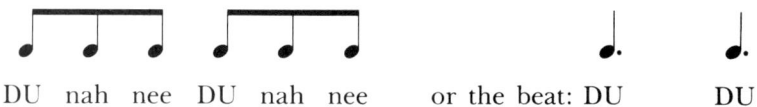

DU nah nee   DU nah nee   or the beat: DU   DU

♪ **Perform** ♪
"The Du Nah Nee Swing"

Only two fundamental divisions of beats occur in music: the duple division, which you know as Du nay, and the triple division, which sounds like, *Du nah nee*. Turn to "The Du Nah Nee Swing" in the Rap section of the Songbook and practice speaking and tapping the rhythms at the top of the page. Remember to keep a steady beat with your foot as you tap, speak, and triple rhythms.

Do not stumble over the sixteenth notes when speaking the Du nah nee rhythm syllables. The quick sound of "te" is used exactly as it was used with the Du nay (duple) division of the beat. When you see and speak the sixteenth notes, it should feel natural, somewhat like when you call someone and change the name: "Tom, Tom, Tommy." The following example shows how this might look in musical notation. Other examples are given here as well.

Du   nah   nee - te

At this point, it would be wise to compare the duple and triple beat divisions. When the beat is a quarter note, it is divided in two, sounding Du nay. The following example shows a familiar rhythm.

When the beat is triple, it is easily divided into three parts, sounding Du nah nee. In this case, the beat is a dotted quarter note. A familiar rhythm looks like this:

Designating whether the meter (or division of the beat) is duple or triple is accomplished with either a note value or a number in the lower part of the meter signature. If you look through the Songbook, all the meter signatures having a quarter note on the bottom are a duple division of the beat; those having a dotted quarter note are a triple division of the beat. In some books numbers are used to designate duple or triple. A lower number of 4 (or 2) denotes duple; an 8 denotes triple.

When you start to perform a song, you must check the meter signature. To obtain a secure feeling of the basic timing for a song, quickly think through the following examples.

Then think:

Du nah nee Du nah nee

Du (n) nee Du (n) nee

In some music books the meter signature for the triple beat division is $\frac{6}{8}$, which tells you that each measure contains six eighth notes. Look at the first measure of the song "Over the River" (Song 12), and count it: 1-2-3-4-5-6. Although this is technically correct, most songs with a $\frac{6}{8}$ meter are actually felt with a strong sense of two dotted quarter beats per measure. When you hear or perform "Row, Row, Row Your Boat," the dotted quarter beat is obvious, even in the two measures with all eighth notes: "merrily, merrily, merrily, merrily." When the six eighth notes are counted, the rhythm tends to be labored and loses the natural flow of two strong beats. Compare the following three lines by speaking and tapping each one several times:

Du	nah	nee	Du	nah	nee	Du	nah	nee	Du	nah	nee
mer-	ri-	ly,	mer-	ri-	ly,	mer-	ri-	ly,	mer-	ri-	ly
1	2	3	4	5	6	1	2	3	4	5	6

It is interesting to note that an increasing number of songbooks are using the triple feeling meter signature: $\frac{2}{}$..

Another good way to practice feeling the difference between the duple and triple beat feeling is to sing or speak the first phrase of "Over the River" (Song 12) and then "Simple Gifts" (Song 13) using rhythm syllables. Alternate the two meters back and forth until you feel the distinct difference.

Look at "Home on the Range" (Song 15) and determine whether the meter is duple or triple. Try reading the rhythm. A couple of patterns in the song have been written out in rhythm syllables in the Introducing section. After you practice these carefully, read the rhythm of the whole song. Practice the song on the recorder.

You must learn the D7 chord before attempting the guitar accompaniment. Practice the following progression before you try to play and sing the song.

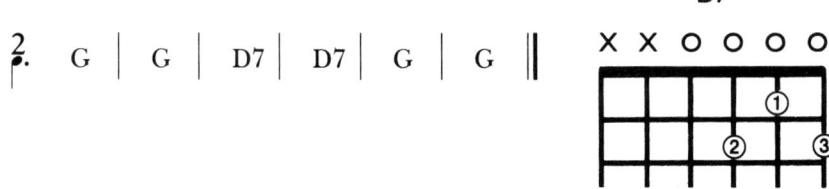

A two-part recorder descant is provided below Song 15 in the Songbook. You will need to be able to play the E on the fourth space of the staff (high E). Illustrated below are two good fingerings for this pitch. The first example shows a "half-closed" thumb hole, but you may use the fingering that is easier for you.

♪ **Perform** ♪
"Home on the Range"
Song 15

Divide the class into four groups. Three groups will play recorder parts (one melody and two descant parts), and one group will sing and accompany the song on the guitar. Pay attention to the correct balance of parts.

What You Have Experienced in This Encounter

The E7 guitar chord
The triple beat feeling
The D7 guitar chord
High E on the recorder

To Further Your Understanding

1. Practice "The Du Nah Nee Swing" in the Rap section of your Songbook.
2. Practice Songs 12 and 15.
3. Practice the E7 and D7 chords on the guitar.
4. Look at several songs in the Songbook and determine the beats (quarter beat or dotted quarter beat) and their divisions, either the Du nay or the Du nah nee sounds.
5. To help you recall the various rhythms that are possible when the beat is a dotted quarter, see if you can remember the examples used in "The Du Nah Nee Swing." For example, your first response might be three eighth notes.

   a.   e.
   b.   f.
   c.   g.
   d.   h.

6. Write in the rhythm syllables for each of the following examples and then practice playing them on your recorder (using any one or two pitches). Be sure to check the meter signature before you start. Remember, if the note value in the meter signature is a dotted quarter note, you will be in the Du nah nee family.

7. Notate an eight-measure example of rhythm in $\frac{2}{p.}$ meter. Write in the rhythm syllables.

_____

8. Notate an eight-measure example of rhythm in $\frac{2}{p}$ meter. Write in the rhythm syllables.

_____

IMPROVING YOUR PERFORMANCE 3

This encounter presents some miscellaneous ideas about how to improve the overall sound of your performances. These ideas apply to your own playing as well as the playing of the performers you will someday be leading.

TIP ONE

Given the same performer, an in-tune instrument will sound better than an out-of-tune instrument. This statement seems so basic that you may wonder why it needs to be discussed at all. Yet many people do not recognize that if a problem exists, it is not necessarily the fault of the performer or the instrument; the preparation (or lack of preparation) for the performance may be to blame. Before experienced performers begin to play music on an instrument, they usually, by habit, play a few isolated pitches to check the tuning. If the instrument is out of tune, time is taken to tune it. Beginners are very different—they often begin playing without first trying their instruments. This lack of preparation (tuning) increases the likelihood of an amateur sound. A good habit to establish is always tuning your instrument before playing.

Tuning the Guitar

To tune the guitar, you must start with a pitch source. Any instrument that produces an accurate pitch will work. The guitarist often uses a piano or a pitch pipe. For your purposes, a recorder can provide the necessary pitch. Play a low E (notated on page 108) on your recorder. This is the pitch to which the lowest-pitched string on your guitar should be tuned. (The lowest string is the thickest, also called the sixth string.) Play low E on the recorder, then play the sixth string on the guitar. The string should sound exactly one octave lower than the recorder. If they do not sound alike, turn the appropriate tuning peg on the guitar neck either clockwise or counterclockwise until the pitches match. The remaining strings are tuned to the sixth string, so be sure it is in tune before proceeding.

Once the sixth string is in tune, move your finger up to the space above the fourth fret (this is actually called "stopping the string *at* the fifth fret"). Stop the low string at this point. This pitch should match the fifth string in open position (see Figure 1). If not, change the pitch of the *fifth* string (not the sixth, which is already in tune) until the pitches match. Repeat this procedure for every string except the second string. When the second string is open, it should match the third string stopped at the fourth fret (see Figure 2).

Figure 1   **Figure 2**

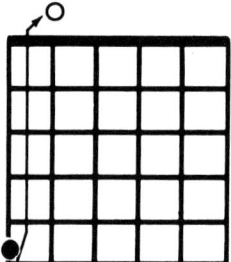   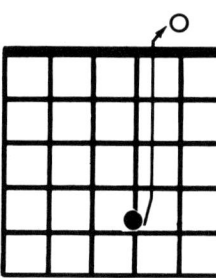

The entire tuning process is depicted in Figure 3.

Figure 3

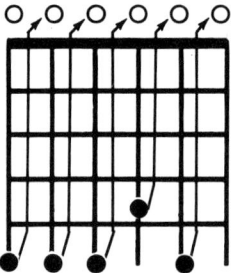

Tuning the guitar takes time at first. Like most music skills, you will become more adept with time and practice. To achieve this important skill, you should begin each practice session with tuning.

Tuning the Recorder

Unlike the guitar, an out-of-tune recorder will sound just fine when playing by itself. This is because a recorder will always be in tune with itself. However, it may be out of tune with other instruments or with other recorders. Fortunately, the recorder can also be tuned. This fact is especially important when a group of individuals are playing together in an ensemble. To tune a recorder, slightly pull the mouthpiece out of the body to make the pitch lower. Push the body into the recorder to make the pitch higher.

A Sense of Leadership

Your musical skills should become "second nature" to you before you perform with or for a group. When you begin to feel comfortable singing and playing instruments, you are probably performing with some sense of leadership. This is very important when you are the accompanist or when you are the leader. What does it mean to show a sense of leadership as you perform? Consider what you see happening when someone in any kind of situation is in command. The person functions automatically and at the same time gives the impression of "reaching out" to the group as if to lead or guide. This is often demonstrated through posture, facial expression, and especially eye contact. There are other, more obvious ways to demonstrate a sense of leadership, including enunciation, projection, and cueing.

Enunciation and Projection

In a good, lively song performance everyone communicates with each other through the words of the song. It is unusual to see performers mumbling the words. Yet when learning and practicing musical skills, it is easy to forget to enunciate the words clearly and project the singing voice and/or the instrument playing. Good singing requires good breath control. Many people who think they can't sing well could improve their skill by breathing deeply, enunciating more exactly and precisely, and projecting their voices. Enunciation and projection *will* result in a sense of leadership.

Cueing a Group

"Cueing" occurs *before* something is begun. You certainly have noticed how important it is for your teacher to "cue in" the group to start a song. Whenever two or more persons begin a task together, someone must signal (or cue) the start. When performing music, the leader must cue the group. Sometimes this is done by conducting or by a simple gesture of the hand and "ready sing." You have already learned to do this when you practiced adding introductions to songs. Sometimes a slight nod of the head or a signal with the eyes also cues in the group.

TIP TWO
The cue is actually the signal for the singers and instrumentalists to take a breath and then begin. The cue occurs on the beat, just before the beginning of the music.

You can practice cueing by asking a class member to recite Lincoln's Gettysburg Address on your signal. Try different ways to "cue" the person to begin. (Your signal, or cue, can also determine how fast or slow and how loud or soft to speak.)

Another aspect of cueing that is often ignored is the leader's preparation before cueing the group. For example, if you want to lead a group in singing "Take Me Out to the Ball Game," you must *think through* and cue yourself before you give any signals to the group. Before leading the group, you should determine the following:

What is the starting pitch? Does the group have it?
Does it begin on a downbeat or an upbeat?
How fast or slow should it go?
What is the spirit or mood of the music?
How does it begin (words, pitches, rhythm)?

As you gain experience leading groups, all this thinking occurs spontaneously, especially if the song is well known. Most of the preceding considerations are answered unconsciously, but none should be ignored.

Finger Picking on the Guitar

One delightful way to improve your guitar playing is through a technique called finger picking. This is a right-hand technique in which the thumb, index, middle, and ring fingers pluck individual pitches of a given chord on the subdivision of the beat.

In this technique (diagrammed in Figure 4) the index finger (i) always plucks the third string, regardless of the chord being played. The middle finger (m) always plays the second string, and the ring finger (r) always plays the first string. The thumb (T) is the only finger of the right hand that moves. It always plays the lowest pitch of the chord, which is the lowest string played. Of course, this changes according to chord being played.

Figure 4

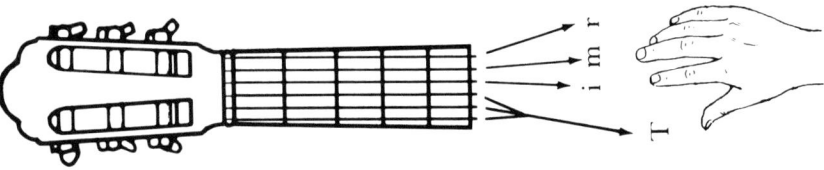

The proper hand position for finger picking is shown in Figure 5. Your hand should be placed so that the fingers are pointing toward the floor; curve them slightly until they rest on their assigned string. The thumb should be pointed toward the head of the guitar.

Figure 5

The following patterns are standard finger-picking progressions. Be sure to use the pattern intended for the meter of the song you are playing.

Duple subdivision of beat:

two or four beats per measure:

three beats per measure:

Triple subdivision of beat:

two beats per measure:

Practice these patterns. Although they feel awkward at first, with practice you will be able to play them in a song such as "Five Hundred Miles" (Song 22) or "Greensleeves" (Song 17).

MUSICAL ENCOUNTER 19
CONSTRUCTING CHORDS FOR SONGS

Introducing

Major and minor chords
Scale functions within chords
Chord functions within a key

What You Will Need

Your Songbook
A recorder
A guitar

Many of the songs for guitar encountered so far have used three different *types* of chords. Besides the pitch name, certain chords have been labelled major (e.g., G Major), minor (e.g., A minor), or seventh (e.g., E7) chords. Other chords have been labelled only by their pitch name (e.g., D). This encounter explains the differences and functions of these various types of chords.

A chord is any combination of three or more different pitches. Technically, any combination of pitches therefore can be called a chord. For example, if you strum all six strings of the guitar without stopping any of them on the frets, this is a chord. Similarly, if eight resonator bells are selected at random and simultaneously played, this also is considered a chord.

All chords are not created equal. The most common types of chords are called *triads*. These are chords having only three separate pitches. Furthermore, the three pitches must be a set distance apart, called a third.

This distance of a third can rightly be called the basic building block of Western harmony. It is important to understand thirds because almost all harmony, not just triads, are based on them.

It is easy to find a pair of pitches that are a third apart. Simply remove all sharps and flats from the pitch alphabet, pick any letter name, and count up three. The first and third pitches are a third apart as shown below. A and C are said to be the *interval* of a third apart, as are E and G, B and D, and F and A. To determine the basic interval of a third, it is not necessary to include accidentals. When measuring thirds, do remember to count the pitch you start on as "1."

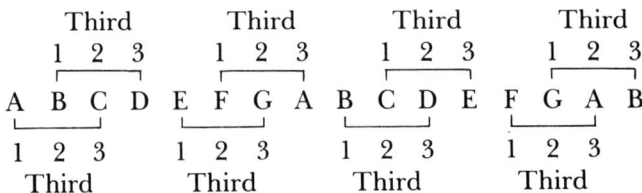

Thirds are easy to see on a staff because both notes are either on a line or a space with only one line or space between them.

Thirds

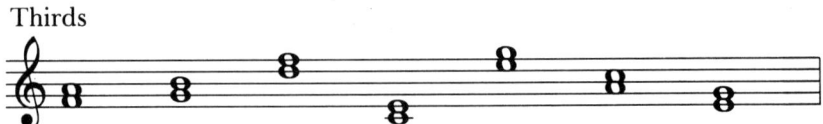

The two types of thirds are *major* and *minor*. The distance between the bottom and top notes in an interval of a major third is two whole steps. The distance between the bottom and top notes in an interval of a minor third is one and one-half steps.

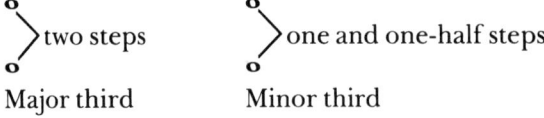

To build, or *construct,* a major or minor interval, you must include the appropriate sharps or flats. This requires that you use the complete pitch alphabet. The following diagram shows some major and minor thirds. (Note that major intervals are bracketed above the staff, minor intervals below the staff.)

Major thirds:

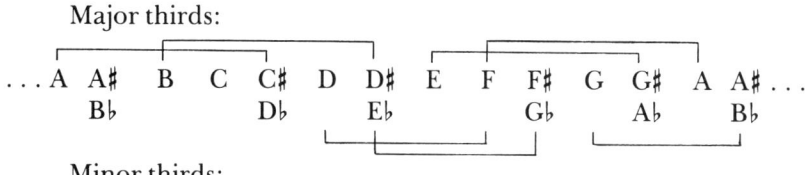

Minor thirds:

When these intervals are notated on the staff, it becomes obvious whether to call a pitch by its sharp or flat name. Simply remember that a third is always notated with both pitches on either lines or spaces. One pitch will never be on a line and the other on a space; this just can't happen. Choose the enharmonic that follows this rule.

On the staff below, identify the major and minor thirds. Play some of these intervals with a partner on your recorders. Although both types of thirds sound "good" to your ear, they should also sound different. Combining these two intervals or sounds ultimately creates most harmony. In fact, the third is so fundamental to all Western harmony that the entire harmonic system used in Western civilization is called *tertian harmony*.

(Answers: Major thirds are 1, 4, 6; minor thirds are 2, 3, 5)

A triad is formed when two thirds of any kind are combined. Thirds are combined by moving up a third from a given pitch and then using this new pitch as the starting point for another third. One possible combination is depicted in the following example.

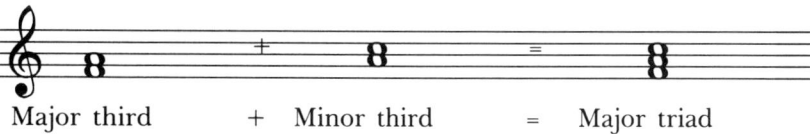

Major third   + Minor third   = Major triad

Only four possible combinations of major and minor thirds exist. These four combinations, which are depicted on page 116, produce the four basic types of triads: major, minor, augmented, and diminished. The standard abbreviations for these chords are M, m, Aug (or +), and dim (or °).

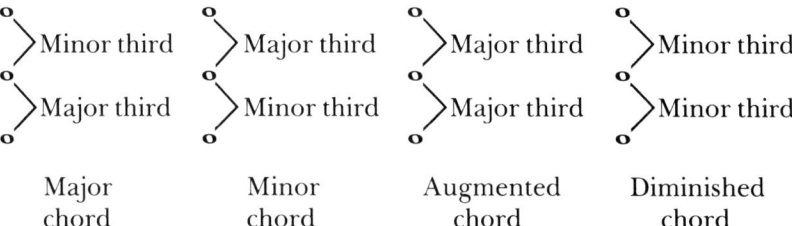

The combinations depicted above can be thought of as "formulas" or "recipes" for constructing each type of chord. The two most common formulas, those for major and minor triads, are easy to remember because they are the reverse of one another with the bottom third defining the type of chord. The other two chords, augmented and diminished, are fairly rare but are included here in case you do come across one.

Although it is not necessary to know the individual pitches in a chord to play it on the guitar, this is not true of other instruments. For example, if you want to play the three pitches of the D chord (or triad) on the resonator bells or piano, you must know the names of the pitches. Likewise, if three recorder players want to play the chords of a song, they must calculate the notes in each chord, each player responsible for playing only one of the three pitches.

To find the pitches in a chord, simply follow the steps provided here. For each step, four chords are built as examples.

Step 1: Notate the root of the chord. The *root pitch* is always the name of the chord. For example, the root of A Major is the pitch A; the root of G minor is the pitch G; the root of D diminished is the pitch D; and the root of F Augmented is pitch F.

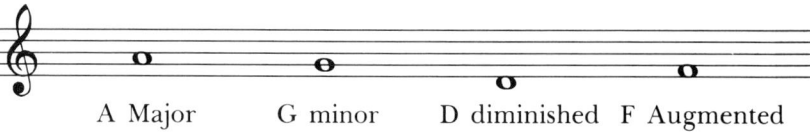

Step 2: Draw two more notes above each root. If the root pitch is on a space, the upper two pitches must be on spaces. Likewise, if the root is on a line, the upper two notes must be on lines.

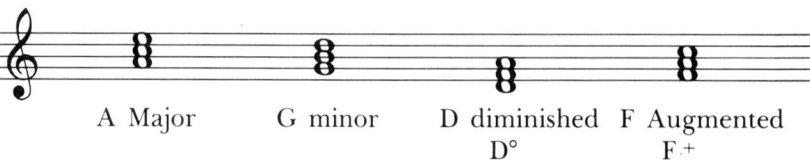

Step 3: Choose the appropriate "formula" of whole and half steps that corresponds with the type of chord you are building. For example, if you are building a minor chord, you will choose the formula for whole and half steps, which is displayed below. A very important point to remember is that a chord is assumed to be a major chord if no designation is noted after a root name (e.g., the "G chord").

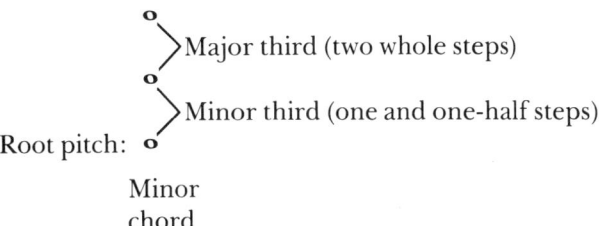

Root pitch:

Minor
chord

Step 4: Add any necessary accidentals to your triad to make it fit the formula. It is very important to realize that you cannot move any of the pitches on your staff. The only alterations that can be made are through the use of accidentals.

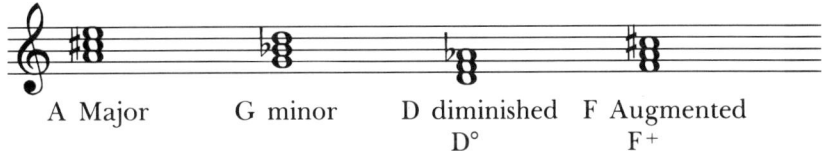

A Major   G minor   D diminished   F Augmented
                                                  D°   F+

That's it. You have found the pitches for each of these chords.

You now can find the individual pitches of any three-note chord. However, some chords have more than three pitches. It is easy to find these additional pitches, because almost everything in tertian harmony is based on thirds. If the chord has a seven (7) after it (as in "A7"), this simply means there is an added pitch in this chord that is the interval of a seventh above the root. (Although other extended chords will not be discussed in this book, any time a number occurs after the root name, the same logic applies. Thus, if a "9" occurs after the chord name, you will know that an added pitch is a ninth above the root; an "11" after the chord name indicates an added pitch an eleventh above the root; and a "13" indicates a pitch a thirteenth above the root.)

This may sound confusing, but it is actually quite easy to do. For example, after building a chord using the steps just given, you decide to make it into a seventh chord. You accomplish this simply by adding one more pitch on top of the chord (see the following example); for a ninth, add two more pitches. If the original three notes are on lines, the new notes also must be on lines; if the original notes are on spaces, the new notes also must be on spaces.

This system works because of tertian harmony. Each time another pitch is added by this method, it is automatically in the interval of a third. Your only responsibility is to ensure that the new chord follows the pattern of major/minor thirds (below) by adding accidentals if necessary.

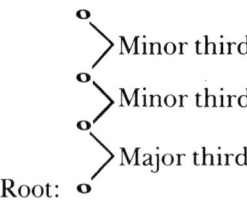

♪ **Perform** ♪
"Bicycle Built for Two"
Song 21

Try the following activity to apply this new skill of building chords. Divide the class into groups and have each group find the pitches for a chord in "Bicycle Built for Two" (Song 21). Once all the chords have been analyzed, have each group notate the individual pitches for their chord on the board. Assign part of the class to perform the bottom notes of each chord on their recorders. Another group plays the second notes, a third group plays third notes, and a fourth group the fourth notes. Play the pitches continuously until the next chord is reached. Reserve some class members for singing, or playing, the melody.

Once the class can perform the chords of this song on the recorder, try making it more interesting by playing the harmony in the rhythm notated in the following example.

♪ **Perform** ♪
"Greensleeves"
Song 17

After the class is comfortable with their performances, try the following activity for a real challenge. Analyze the chords for "Greensleeves" (Song 17). Then assign each member of the class a resonator bell that corresponds to a pitch occurring in the chords. As the class sings the melody, each person must decide if their bell (pitch) is present in the chord being played. If done correctly, this will sound quite pretty.

Scale Functions Within Chords

The seventh chord is important and therefore worthy of further investigation. When introductions were discussed in Encounter 17, the importance of the V7 chord was emphasized. The introductions used in that encounter generally ended with the V7 chord because of its "pulling tendency" toward the I chord. You are now ready to see why the pulling tendency of this seventh chord exists.

When you learned to build scales in Encounter 10, you also learned about certain psychological properties of a scale. These properties amounted to the apparent "pulling tendencies" of certain pitches to other pitches in the scale. Specifically, these tendencies were noted as follows:

Re   pulls to Do
Ti   pulls to Do
Sol   pulls to Do
Fa   pulls to Mi

These tendencies are graphically depicted in the following example.

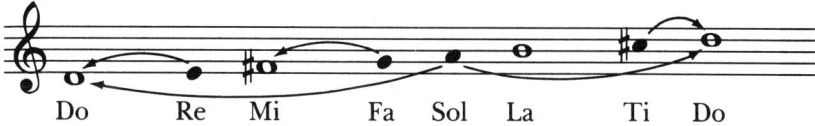

If all the pitches having a pulling tendency in a given scale were combined, they would produce a seventh chord constructed on the fifth degree of the scale, the V7 chord. If the pitches of the V7 chord are rearranged in thirds, they are A, C♯, E, and G.

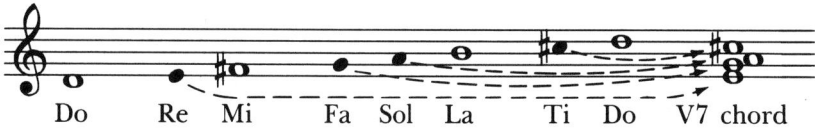

If all the resolution pitches of a given scale were combined, they would produce the I chord (with one pitch missing).

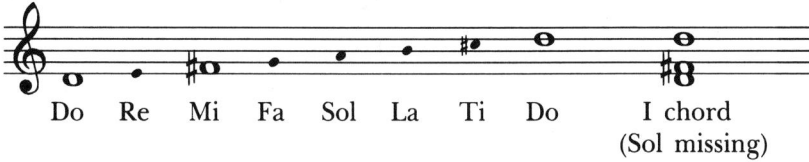

Because of the inherent properties of the major scale, the harmony (which is based on the scale) has the same psychological characteristics. Thus, the V7 chord in any key will always have a "pulling tendency" to the I, or tonic, chord in that key.

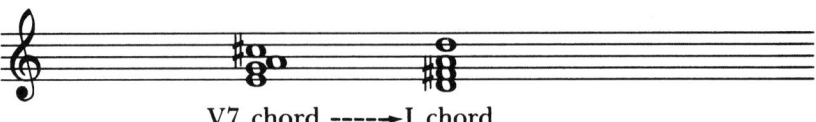

V7 chord -----→ I chord

As you saw in the construction of introductions, this V7 to I relationship can be a very powerful and important musical force. It is also extremely useful in writing songs (or any type of music).

A Shortcut to Finding Chord Pitches

As you recall, the scale is perhaps the most fundamental aspect of pitch in music. From the previous discussion of seventh chords, you can see that scale functions influence the harmony of music as much as they do the melody. This fact can be very useful in determining the individual pitches of a piece of music.

In a given key the harmony pitches are determined by the key scale much like the melody pitches are. Therefore, although exceptions do exist, the chords will primarily be comprised of the seven pitches of the scale. This makes chord construction very easy.

To find the pitches in the chords of a song (when the key is known), simply notate the scale as shown:

Once the scale is notated, draw a triad on top of every pitch. Then put in the accidentals dictated by the key signature of the song as shown:

You have just constructed the chords of this scale. In any major scale these chords will always follow a set pattern of major, minor, and diminished chords.

I			IV	V			are always Major
	ii	iii			vi		are always minor
						vii	is always diminished

It is important to note that many songs will use chords that are "outside the key." If a chord in a song does not follow the above rule, you can find the individual pitches by constructing the chord according to the formulas. An example of this can be found in Song 24 in the key of D Major. If the scale and chords are constructed, you can see that an E minor chord should be in the song (see below). Instead, the song has an E7 chord. This chord is borrowed from another key and will need to be constructed according to the formula for seventh chords described earlier.

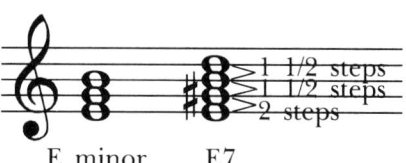

E minor   E7

This shortcut method may seem confusing. After using it a few times, however, you will probably find it easier than the other method. The hardest part is finding the exceptions to the rules, but few of these generally occur in a given song. It is important to understand that either method works equally well. Feel free to use the one that is most comfortable for you.

What You Have Experienced in This Encounter

Major and minor chords
Scale functions within chords
Chord functions within a key

To Further Your Understanding

1. Add Song 21 to your rehearsal grid.
2. Complete "Introducing Song 21."
3. Notate the individual pitches that comprise each of the designated chords below:

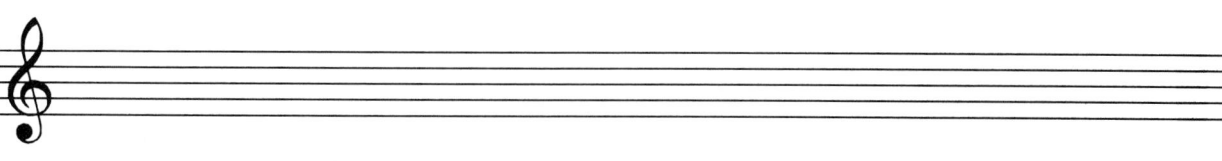

A minor   F Major   D Major   A Major

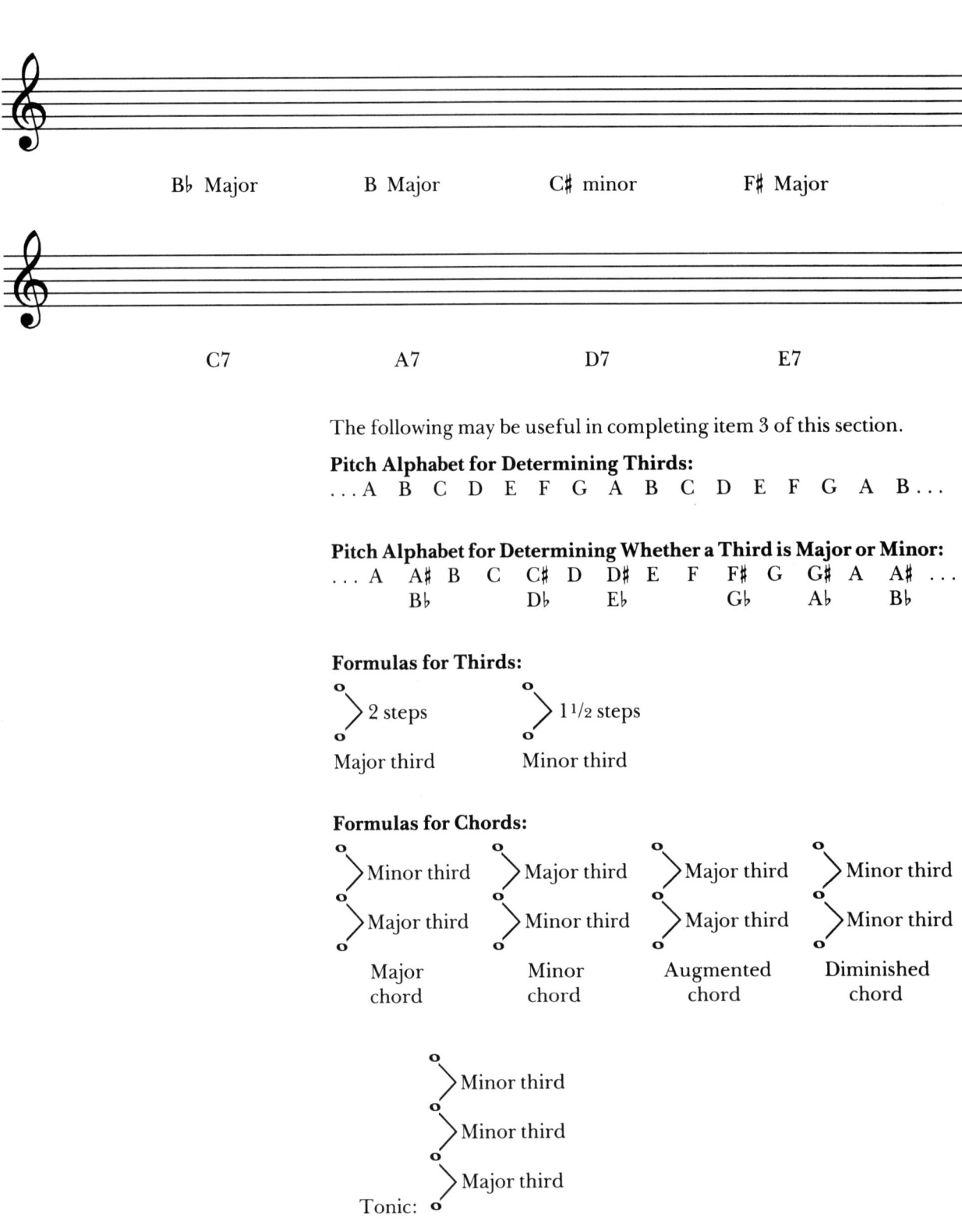

Bb Major   B Major   C# minor   F# Major

C7   A7   D7   E7

The following may be useful in completing item 3 of this section.

Pitch Alphabet for Determining Thirds:
...A   B   C   D   E   F   G   A   B   C   D   E   F   G   A   B...

Pitch Alphabet for Determining Whether a Third is Major or Minor:
...A   A#   B   C   C#   D   D#   E   F   F#   G   G#   A   A# ...
    Bb   Db   Eb   Gb   Ab   Bb

Formulas for Thirds:

2 steps   1 1/2 steps

Major third   Minor third

Formulas for Chords:

Minor third   Major third   Major third   Minor third

Major third   Minor third   Major third   Minor third

Major   Minor   Augmented   Diminished
chord   chord   chord   chord

Minor third

Minor third

Major third

Tonic:

Seventh chord

MUSICAL ENCOUNTER **20**
TRANSPOSING A MELODY

Introducing

Transposing a melody from one key to another
Recorder pitches: F♮, B♭, middle C
First and second endings
A round—a musical form

What You Will Need

A recorder

Begin this encounter by learning to play "Aura Lea," (Song 18) on the recorder. Notice from the key of the song that the scale will be F, G, A, B♭, C, D, E, F. So far you have played in keys that use an F♯ and B♮. Study the recorder fingerings below for the new pitches needed to play in the key of F, and practice the following example so that you will feel comfortable playing these new pitches.

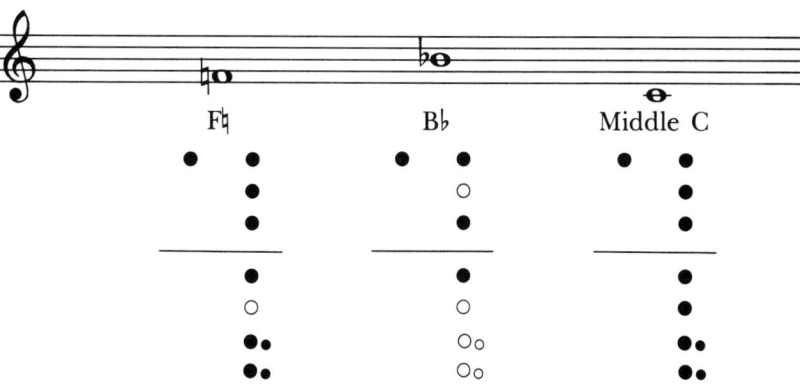

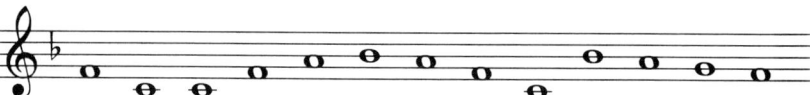

Before you begin to play the song, you must be aware of a shorthand way of notating repeated parts in a song. Read through the first line of "Aura Lea" until you see the repeat sign. Notice that the last measure you played was marked "1.," meaning the first ending. Now go back to the beginning to play the repeat. Skip over the measure marked as the first ending, and play the measure marked "2.," meaning the second ending. These notations are shown below.

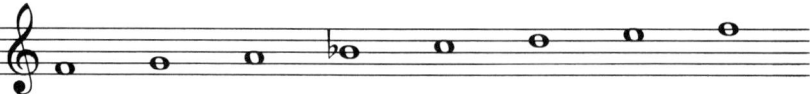

♪ **Perform** *p*
"Aura Lea"
Song 18
on the recorder

Double check what you played, by reading through the words for the first two lines of the song as you should have performed them.

As the blackbird in the spring, 'Neath the willow tree,
Sat and piped, I heard him sing, Singing Aura Lea.

Suppose you want to play this song in the key of G so that it can be accompanied on the guitar. (Guitar chords in the key of G are much easier than in the key of F.) In an earlier encounter you learned to transpose chords from one key to another. Now you will *transpose a melody* from one key to another so that you can play it in the new key on the recorder. You may also occasionally want to transpose a song to a more comfortable key for singing.

The principle for transposing a melody is the same as for transposing chords, but the steps are slightly different. Follow the steps below as "Aura Lea" is transposed from the key of F Major to the key of G Major.

Step 1: Write the scale for the key the song is in (F Major) before you begin to transpose.

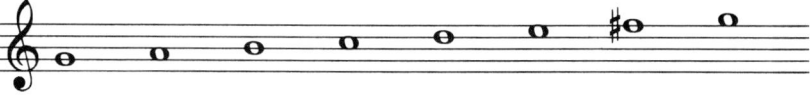

Step 2: Write the scale for the key to which you are transposing (G Major).

Step 3: Draw lines connecting the corresponding scale degrees in each key.

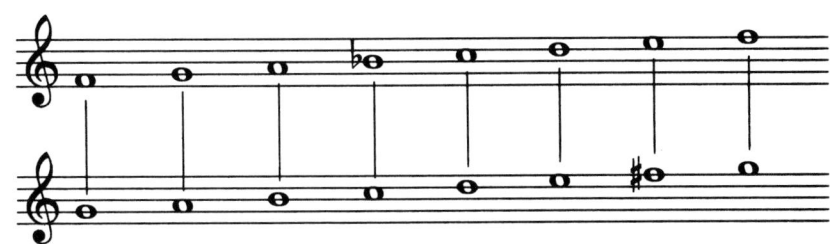

Step 4: Refer to the scale drawn for Step 3 as you rewrite the song, converting each pitch to the corresponding pitch in the new key. When rewriting, remember that *the contour (or shape) of the melody must remain the same.* This may mean that some pitches will be in a different octave than the original scale drawn in Step 2. The first two measures of "Aura Lea" are shown below as an example.

Key of F

Key of G

This procedure seems to take longer to explain than it does to accomplish. Once you realize how it works, it is not difficult. However, there is a shorthand method. Once again, follow these steps:

Step 1: Determine the original key; name the tonic note.
Step 2: Determine the new key; name its tonic note.
Step 3: Decide whether you need to move up or down to transpose, and how many places this must occur on the staff (see the example below).

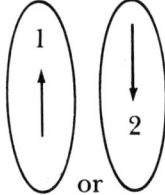

Step 4: Move each pitch in the song up or down the determined number of places on the staff.

For example, if you transpose from F Major to G Major, the tonic notes are F and G, respectively. In this case simply move each pitch *up* one place on the staff. If the key signature is there, or you know what it is, the accidentals will be in place. Following are some more examples.

If you transpose from the key of E to the key of C, the tonic notes are E and C, respectively. In this case move *down* two places on the staff. The following example shows two transpositions. The first is from the key of D. If you transpose from the key of D to the key of E♭, the tonic notes are D and E♭. Move *up* one place on the staff. The second transposition shown is from the key of C. If you transpose from the key of C to the key of F, the tonic notes are C and F. Move *up* three places on the staff.

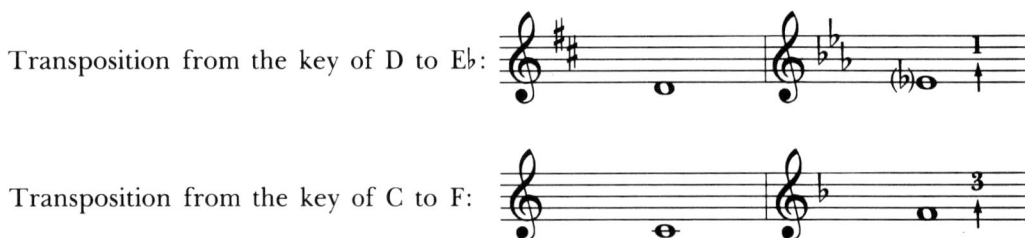

Transposition from the key of D to E♭:

Transposition from the key of C to F:

♪ **Perform** *f*
"Music Alone Shall Live"
Song 10
on the recorder

To complete this encounter, transpose Song 10, "Music Alone Shall Live," to the key of G Major. Practice it in the new key, and then the whole class can play it in a round. Be sure to transpose the chords also, so that the round can be accompanied on the guitar or Autoharp.

You will notice that the lines of Song 10 have been numbered 1, 2, and 3. This identifies the song as a round. The other clue that this song can be performed in a round is the harmony (designated by the chords above the melody). When the harmony for each line is the same, the song can be performed in a round. Divide the class into three groups. Group one begins; as they start the second line of the song, group two begins the song. When group two starts the second line, group three starts at the beginning of the song.

Group 1	Line 1	Line 2	Line 3	. . . .
Group 2		Line 1	Line 2	Line 3 . . . .
Group 3			Line 1	Line 2 Line 3 . . . .

A round usually is performed two or three times, and the effect is that of hearing the melody go "round and round" the group.

What You Have Experienced in This Encounter

New pitches on the recorder: F♮, B♭, and middle C
Notating repetition in music, using first and second endings
Transposing melodies
A round—a musical form

To Further Your Understanding

1. Practice Song 18.
2. Transpose Song 11 to the key of C Major.
3. Transpose Song 6 to the key of F Major.
4. Play transposed Songs 11 and 6 on your recorder.

MUSICAL ENCOUNTER 21
MINOR SCALES

Introducing

Minor scales
Naming a minor key from the key signature
Determining whether a song key is major or minor
Tuning up for singing a minor song
Ambiguity of minor

What You Will Need

Your Songbook
A recorder
A guitar

An earlier encounter looked at the following pulling tendencies, which are inherent in the structure of the major scale.

Re pulls toward Do
Ti pulls toward Do
Sol pulls toward Do
Fa pulls toward Mi

These pulling tendencies in the F major scale are shown below.

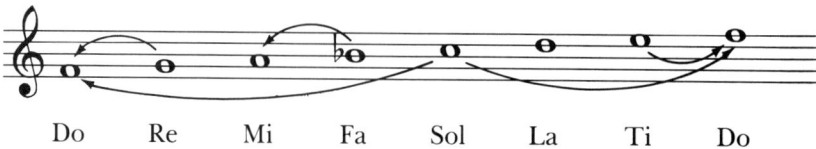

Do   Re   Mi   Fa   Sol   La   Ti   Do

The most important point to note about these tendencies for the discussion that follows is that the structure of this scale evokes a response within you. You can feel a tendency toward certain notes, sometimes even physically.

In the same way, altering the major scale structure evokes a different response. If the third, sixth, and seventh degrees of a scale are lowered, the result evokes a certain feeling. To test this result, alter the D Major scale in the following example by lowering Mi, La and Ti one-half step each.

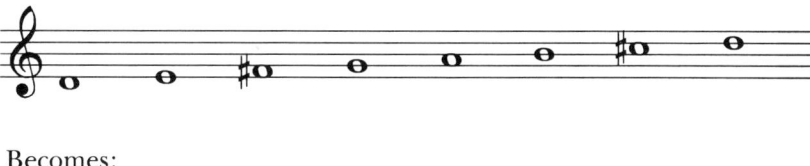

Becomes:

Now play "Are You Sleeping?" (Song 2) on the recorder, first using the pitches of the regular D Major (first example) and then the pitches of the altered D Major (second example).

Example 1

"Are You Sleeping?" in D Major

Example 2

"Are You Sleeping?" in altered D Major

You probably noticed a big difference in the two versions. How would you describe this difference? Did you tend to play the two versions of the song at different tempos? With different dynamics? Why?

The "altered scale" you used to play the second version of "Are You Sleeping?" is actually the D *minor scale*. You can tell that it makes the song sound very different. Just like the major scale, the minor scale prompts a certain response from listeners. Some people think that songs using minor scales sound sad. Although this is sometimes true (as in the version of "Are You Sleeping?"), it is certainly an oversimplification of the power of this scale. For example, the song "Drunken Sailor" (Song 8) is in a minor key (i.e., it uses a minor scale), yet this song does not sound sad. Likewise, "Hava Nagila," the Israeli dance song, sounds exciting. It sounds different than if it were in major but does not necessarily sound sad.

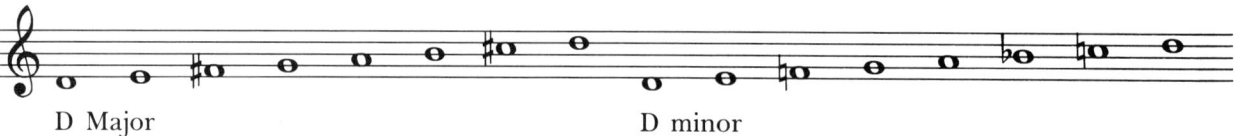

D Major   D minor

Again compare the D Major and D minor scales above. Notice that they both begin and end on the pitch D. This is the "home tone," or tonic, of both of these arrangements of pitches. All of the pitches in either scale will seem to gravitate toward the pitch of D.

Now compare the D minor and F Major scales below.

D minor   F Major

Notice that both of the scales use exactly the same pitches. Since they are built from different tonic pitches, however, the relationships between the notes change.

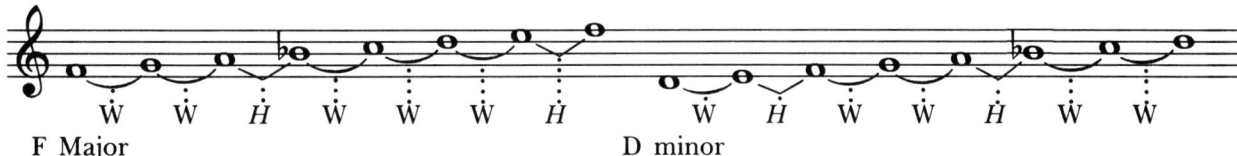

It may seem odd that two scales with the same pitches could sound so different and evoke such different responses. This simply reinforces that fundamental aspect of music, which indicates that the sound relationship between the pitches, not the pitches themselves, are most critical in music. When the pitch relationships of the major scale change, all of the pulling tendencies disappear. In other words, the pitches are identical, only the relationships between them change. The scale therefore sounds different to you.

Since the F Major and D minor scales share the same pitches, they are said to be related. It follows that the two scales also share a key signature. Both F Major and its relative, D minor, use a key signature of one flat.

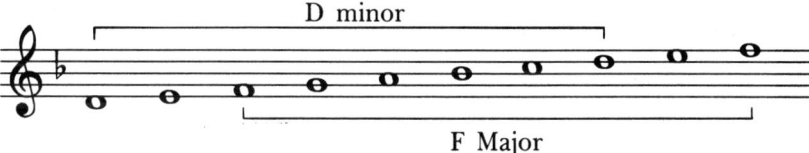

If the key signature and the pitches are the same, how do you know if the song is written in the major or minor key? For the sake of performing, it does not matter. If the music is played as written, the *sound* will indicate either major or minor keys. In fact, this is the best way to tell. If after listening, you are still unsure whether it is major or minor, the next clue comes from looking at the chords. If the song starts and/or ends on the tonic chord of the minor key, it is probably in minor; if it ends on the major tonic, it is probably major. Finally, examine the last note of the song. Again, major tonic equals major key; minor tonic equals minor key.

Listen for this difference in sound as you perform Songs 8, 19, and 20 on the recorder.

♪ **Perform** ♪
"Drunken Sailor"
"Coventry Carol"
and "Theme from
Polovetsian Dances"
Songs 8, 19, and 20
on the recorder

Naming a Minor Key from the Key Signature

In an earlier encounter you learned how to find the name of a major key by looking at the key signature. Once the major key is determined, it is easy to find the name of the minor key. Simply follow this rule: If the major tonic pitch is on a line, the minor tonic pitch (and thus the key name) is on the line below it. If the major tonic is on a space, the minor tonic is on the space below it (see the following example). There are no exceptions to this rule. This rule also can be reversed. If you know the minor tonic, the major tonic is above it.

G Major F Major E Major D Major
E minor D minor C♯ minor B minor

One word of caution should be noted when using this rule: Be sure to remember that the key signature you are investigating is in effect during this process. That is why the relative minor of E Major is C♯ minor and not C minor.

Although this "sharing of pitches" may seem complex, it does have one great advantage. You don't have to learn formulas for constructing minor scales! Just use the formula that you already know for finding the pitches of a major scale. Then arrange them so that they start on the minor tonic instead of on the major tonic.

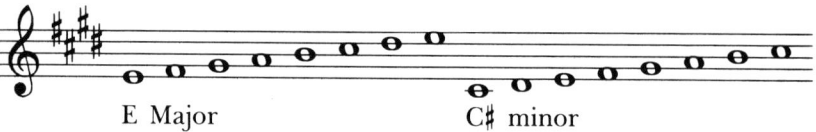

E Major C♯ minor

Determining Whether a Song Key is Major or Minor

The idea of determining whether a piece of music is major or minor often is confusing for beginning musicians. The following chart will help you progress from the known aspects of a song to the unknown aspect—i.e., whether it is in major or minor key. The chart is completed for Songs 6 and 8 from the Songbook. This progression can be used for finding the keys of any songs.

Known	Song 6	Song 8
Key signature:	𝄞♯	𝄞♯
Key of song:	Either G Major or E minor	Either G Major or E minor
Final chord:	G (Major)	Em (E minor)
Final pitch of song:	G	E
By reviewing the evidence, you can establish the following keys:	G Major	E minor

Tuning Up for Singing a Minor Song

You learned to sing the tonal pattern, Do-Mi-Sol-Mi-Do in a major key, stopping on the starting pitch of a song. A similar progression is used in a minor key, but the tonal syllables are not the same. (The tonal patterns of the I chord in minor would actually be La-Do-Mi-Do-La. If you can explain why, you have a complete understanding of the relationship between major and minor scales.) To avoid confusion, it is common for a songleader to sing the appropriate pitches on the syllable "loo" as shown below.

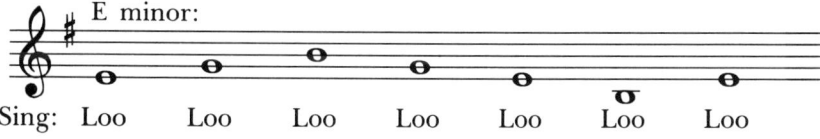

Sing: Loo   Loo   Loo   Loo   Loo   Loo   Loo

It is important that you can hear and sing a tonic chord in minor. Play the Em (E minor) chord on your guitar in a slow tempo. Find the tonic (E) and sing it. Try to sing the pattern above as you play the E minor chord. Repeat this pattern until you feel comfortable with the sound of minor.

The Ambiguity of Minor

Some songs switch back and forth between major and minor. Two common examples are "Greensleeves" (Song 17) and "Erie Canal." Some minor scales borrow tendencies from the major (specifically, the strong Ti-Do pull). Most of this shifting is accomplished through the use of accidentals, not key signatures. Therefore, you will often see many accidentals in a piece of music written in minor. Both of these techniques (switching between major and minor and borrowing from the major key) work to break down the tonality of minor keys. Thus, minor keys often seem much more ambiguous to the ear of the listener than do major keys.

What You Have Experienced in This Encounter

Minor scales
Naming a minor key from the key signature
Determining whether a song key is major or minor
Tuning up for singing a minor song
Ambiguity of minor

To Further Your Understanding

1. Add Songs 19 and 20 to your practice schedule.
2. Practice singing the tonic chord in minor while playing an E minor chord on the guitar.
3. Practice determining whether a song is in major or minor key. Complete the chart for each of the following examples.

Final pitch and chord	Possible keys	Final chord	Final song pitch	Probable key
F				
Em				
Am				
Bm				
B♭				
F♯m				

MUSICAL ENCOUNTER 22
KEYBOARD AWARENESS

Introducing

The pitch alphabet on a keyboard
Creating accompaniments from harmony (chords)

What You Will Need

Access to a piano keyboard, a xylophone, or set of bells

You are able to play melodies and harmony parts on the recorder, rhythm accompaniments on percussion instruments, and chord accompaniments on the guitar and Autoharp. Sometimes a piano, a xylophone, or a set of bells are handy, and you can use them to play exactly the same parts that you have been playing on your recorder. All those fundamentals of music that you now understand can apply to any keyboard instrument.

Keyboard Instruments

Keyboards refer to a family of instruments, including the piano, organ, synthesizer, and all types of bells. Several of these types of bells are named here because you may see them in a school or recreation-type situation. Some xylophones, glockenspiels, and metallophones are not capable of playing the complete pitch alphabet; they have only F♯ and B♭ for accidentals. Children's xylophones are usually only one octave long; others are one and one-half octaves or more in length. Tone bells or resonator bells are individual xylophone bars that can be removed from their case.

Asking individuals to play two or three bells is far less complicated or intimidating than putting a xylophone in front of them. For example, play the ostinato notated below with a song, using only the B, G, and D resonator bells.

Think of the piano, synthesizer, and organ as the most common keyboard instruments. When you look at them, you are seeing the same pitch alphabet that you already know. The black keys are the sharps and flats, or accidentals. It is wise to note two things as you study the keyboard:

1. The pattern of two black keys plus three black keys that is repeated over and over as you move from one octave to another
2. The natural half steps between E and F, B and C

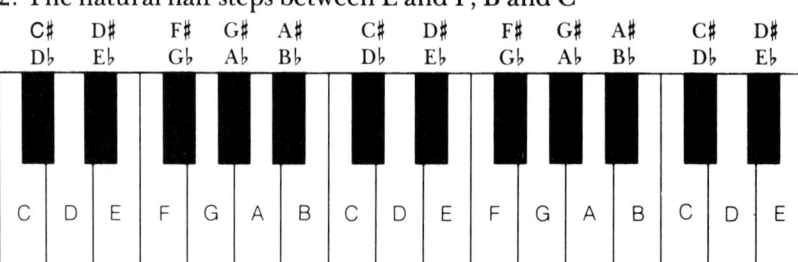

Following are some practice suggestions to help you learn the keyboard and find pitches quickly:

1. Move randomly across the keyboard, playing *and* naming the half steps E and F, B and C. Then choose one or two other pitches (e.g., F and C; F♯ and G), finding, playing, and naming only these. Practice this with many pairs of pitches. Gradually your eyes will begin to recognize where certain pitches are found.
2. To visually connect the keyboard with the written musical notation, play the random pitches in the following exercise at a steady tempo. Each time you repeat this exercise, increase your tempo to challenge your eyes and fingers. (The exercise uses the same pitches you play on your recorder. That means you play what might be sung; the range covers approximately one and one-half octaves. Middle C, which is near the middle of the piano, determines the placement of the other pitches on the staff. The third space (counting from the bottom) is the C above middle C.)

Creating Accompaniments from Harmony (Chords)

Some harmony parts to be played with "Drunken Sailor" (Song 8) are shown in the following example. Try each of the parts on the piano, xylophone, or tone bells. It is possible that Part 2 cannot be played on the particular xylophone you have because of the limited number of bars on the instrument. Try Part 2 on another instrument such as the piano. Divide up the parts in the figure among members of the group and create an ensemble to perform the song.

Your ensemble may consist of:

Part 1: guitar accompaniment with singers
Parts 2, 3, and 4: harmony parts to be played on the recorder, piano, and xylophone

Hopefully, your ensemble performance will be successful. Of course, any successful ensemble must practice together carefully and listen closely to each other for blend and balance. If you listen carefully, you may realize that the harmony parts are created from the chords. When an E minor chord is called for in the first two measures of the ensemble performance, the harmony, or accompaniment, consists of pitches from the Em chord. Likewise, when the D major chord is called for in the third and fourth measures, the harmony consists of D, F♯, and A (the D major chord).

Look at the first measure again. Play the chord root, E, and any rhythm using E, G, and B on the piano. Shown on page 138 is one example for the measures calling for an Em chord. (There could be any number of other rhythm possibilities.) The second measure is an example to use for the measure marked D. Using these two measures as examples and following the chord markings, accompany all of Song 8 on the piano.

Now that you can spell chords, various accompaniments can be added to the songs by playing chord roots and chord pitches in various rhythms. The following principles will guide you as you create more harmony parts to accompany songs on instruments or even to sing.

1. Have a good balance of sound between the melody and the accompaniment.
2. Plan an interesting, but not overpowering, variety of accompaniment parts.
3. Don't use all accompaniment possibilities in one version of the song.

Harmonizing with Voices

You may have found yourself humming along in harmony with some of the accompaniment parts introduced in this encounter. In fact, some of the harmony parts you have learned to create for keyboard instruments also can be sung. The chords in the first four measures of "The Du Nah Nee Swing" (G, Em, Am, D7) establish the harmonic basis for many familiar songs. These songs can be sung while repeating this chord progression over and over on an accompanying instrument, or by humming a part with your voice. If you know the melody to any of the following songs, try singing them while playing the G, Em, Am, D7 chord progression on the guitar. Try to hum a part in the harmony as some of your classmates sing the song.

"I Love the Mountains"	"Blue Moon"
"Can't Help Lovin' That Man"	"Heart and Soul"
"Duke of Earl"	"Silhouettes"

Can you think of other songs? The last line of the harmony will have to be changed to G, Em, Am, D7, G.

What You Have Experienced in This Encounter

The pitch alphabet on a keyboard
Creating accompaniment parts from harmony (chords)

To Further Your Understanding

Using your understanding of how accompaniments grow out of chords, create harmony parts for "This Land is Your Land" (Song 16). You should have one harmony part for recorder, one for resonator bells or xylophone, and a part for the piano. Here is a chart of the chords as they appear in the song to help you get started. Notice that it begins with a pick-up, "This land is." A four-measure introduction is also given for guitar and possibly piano.

Key of D Major:

Introduction   Song

D | G | A7 | D | G | D | A7 | D |

                          | G | D | Em A7 | D ||

MUSICAL ENCOUNTER 23
BRINGING IT ALL TOGETHER
BY PRESENTING A CONCERT

Introducing

Your music to the public
Organizing your band

What You Will Need

Guitars
Recorders
Autoharps
Omnichords
Voices
Most of the knowledge from this book

You have certainly come a long way since Encounter 1 when you first held your guitar. If you are like most students, you probably still wish you were a better musician than you are now. By all means, continue your growth in music. However, now is the time to celebrate the phenomenal progress that you have already made. There is no better way to celebrate than to perform a few songs for others.

Start by dividing the class into small groups, or bands, of individuals. Each band should have between four and eight members. Next, select the music that you want to present. Pick at least three songs or raps from the Songbook or elsewhere that the class members know and can play. Don't forget to review some of the earlier songs that you have learned.

For example, "Rocka My Soul" or "Tom Dooley" will probably seem fairly easy for you now. A rule of thumb for any performance is that it is much better to perform easy music well than to perform difficult music poorly.

After choosing your selections, devise musical arrangements for each song. Compose appropriate introductions, then add percussion and resonator bell parts. Incorporate an ostinato or descant where appropriate. Decide which instruments will add the best "color" to the song. Autoharps, Omnichords, and guitars often blend well together and provide a firm support for singing. Another good support idea is to use the rhythm section from the Omnichord (if you have one) as a complete drum set. Don't be afraid to transpose a song to a key that would be easier to sing or play.

Organizing Your Band

You must choose one person to lead in counting off each song to get the group starting together. This leader also will be the groups' "ears." As such, he or she is responsible for the musical balance of the individual parts. The leader also sets the tempos. You will need to decide as a group which instruments are being played by which band members. Ideally, there should be some switching of instruments.

Successful bands spend their time making music, not talking about what they wish they could do. Practice the songs repeatedly but always with a reason. In other words, be aware of the objective or goal of repeating the song, which usually focuses on areas needing improvement. Remember to keep it simple; simplicity often is the key to effectiveness in band performances.

Decide the order of performance for each band. The bands then perform their three selections in front of the class. It is a good idea to invite friends, roommates, parents, or even another class to hear your performance.

After each group performs their three songs, it is fitting to have a grand finale. An ensemble arrangement of "Ob La Di, Ob La Da" (Song 32) is included in the Songbook for this purpose. It has three separate recorder parts of differing degrees of difficulty, a guitar or Autoharp part, and singing. It is also advisable to add a percussion part to enhance the vitality of the music.

Although you might be nervous while performing, you hopefully will feel a certain amount of excitement and pride in your presentation, and will realize how far you have progressed as a musician. You can see that performing for others is an important milestone for a musician. The concert does not have to be formal; classroom concerts such as this one can establish important goal-directed behavior in students. The feeling of accomplishment after a performance is very special. Hold on to it as long as you can.

To the Future

You have experienced much frustration and, hopefully, just as much joy from these encounters with music. Someday, when you are in charge of a group, it is hoped that you will feel competent and committed to sharing your experiences with others. If you do, then this course and this book have been successful.

What You Have Experienced in This Encounter

Organizing a band
Performing a concert

To Further Your Understanding

Continue your musical growth in whatever capacity you feel comfortable.

NOTES

NOTES

Duple Beat

1. 
2. 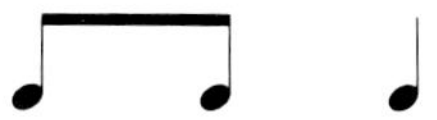
3. 
4. 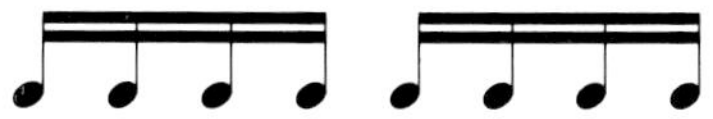
5. 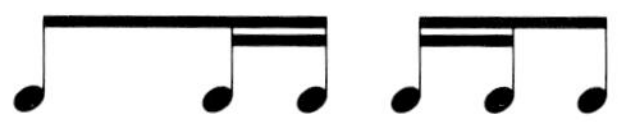
6. 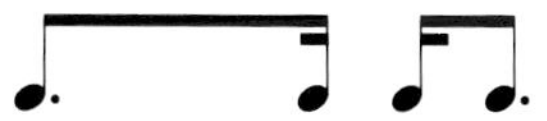
7. 
8. 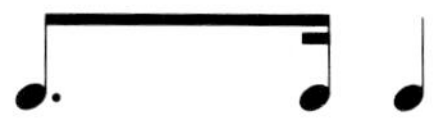

Triple Beat

1. 
2. 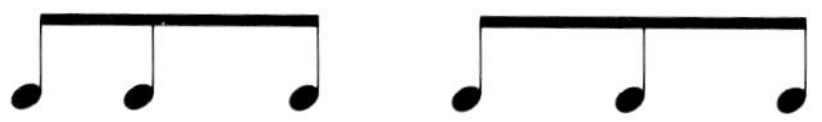
3. 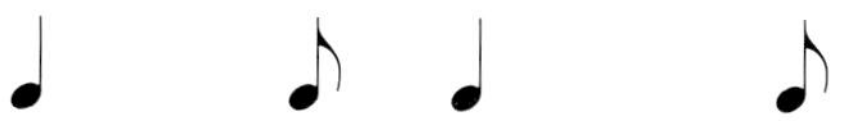
4. 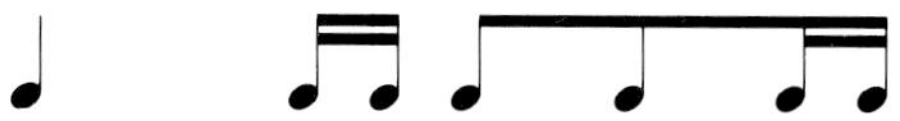
5. 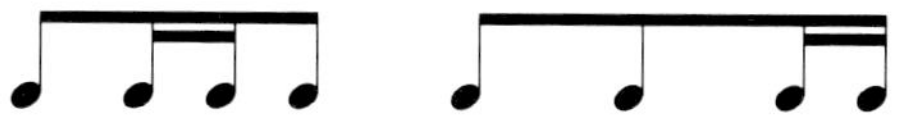
6. 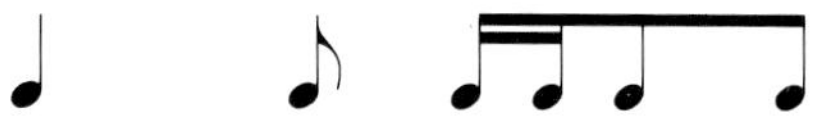
7. 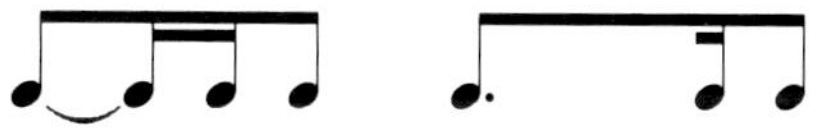
8. 

THE SONGBOOK

Songbook Contents

MORE SONGS TO SING AND PLAY

PART ONE

Each song in this part of the book is introduced with pertinent information about the song. Some of the information becomes more meaningful as you progress through the book. When blanks occur, fill them in with the correct information.

Introducing Song 1: "Row, Row, Row Your Boat"

Key: D Major
Starting pitch: Do (D)
Possible introduction: D / / / | A7 / / / | A7 / / / | D / / /
Count off: 1-2-Ready sing
Meter: 2 (triple division)
Pitch range: This song can be sung as a round with each additional part starting at the beginning of each line.

Song 1: "Row, Row, Row Your Boat"

D / / /
Row, row, row your boat

/ / / /
Gently down the stream _____.

/ / / /
Merrily, Merrily, Merrily, Merrily

/ / / /
Life is but a dream _____.

Introducing Song 2: "Are You Sleeping?"

Key: D Major
Starting pitch: Do (D)
Possible introduction: D / / / | A7 / / / | A7 / / / | D / / /
Count off: 1-2-Ready sing
Meter: 4 (Duple Division)
Expressiveness: Joyously
Pitch range: Good for elementary-age children

Song 2: "Are You Sleeping?"

D	/	/	/	/	/	/	/
Are	you	sleep	- ing?	Are	you	sleep	- ing?

/	/	/	/	/	/	/	/
Bro	- ther	John	___?	Bro	- ther	John	___?

/	/	/	/	/	/	/	/
Morning	bells are	ring	- ing.	Morning	bells are	ring	- ing.

/	/	/	/	/	/	/	/
Ding,	Ding,	Dong	___.	Ding,	Ding,	Dong	___.

Recorder pattern to be performed with Song 1 or 2:

Pitches: A B A B A B A B A B . . . .
Beats: / / / / / / / / / / . . . .

Introducing Song 3: "He's Got the Whole World in His Hands"

Key: D Major
Starting pitch: Sol (A)
Possible introduction: D / / / | A7 / / / | A7 / / / | D / / /
Count off: 1-Ready-Sing
Meter: 4
Structure: Notice that lines one and three are musically identical. The second line is similar in that the rhythm and contour of the melody are identical. Line four is entirely different, therefore the structure is as follows:

A
A'
A
B

When lines are similar, they are denoted with a prime mark ('). Thus the second line in this song is A prime (A').
Expressiveness: Joyously
Pitch range: Good for elementary-age children

Potential trouble spots: The A7 chord in the second to last measure is not held as long as all the other chords in the song. Be ready for a quick change back to D on the word "hands."

Song 3 ···············HE'S GOT THE WHOLE WORLD IN HIS HANDS

2. He's got the wind and the rain in His hands.

3. He's got you and me, brother, in His hands.

4. He's got everybody in His hands.

5. He's got the whole world in His hands.

Introducing Song 4:
"Rocka My Soul"

(Fill in any blanks)
Key: D Major
Starting pitch: Mi (F♯)
Possible introduction: D / / / | D / / / | A7 / / / | A7 / / / |
Count off: 1-2-Ready-Sing
Meter: 4
Structure: _____
Expressiveness: Carefree, happily
Pitch range: Good for elementary-age children

Potential trouble spots:
Remember the D.C. al Fine!
Always strum the steady beat. Do not change the strum in the B section even if you are tempted.

Song 4   ROCKA MY SOUL

Rock - a   my   soul ___   in   the   bo - som   of   A - bra - ham,

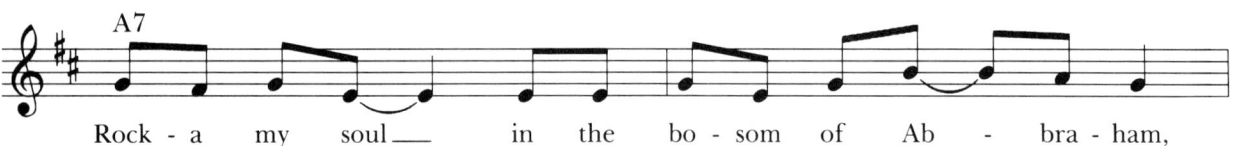

Rock - a   my   soul ___   in   the   bo - som   of   Ab - bra - ham,

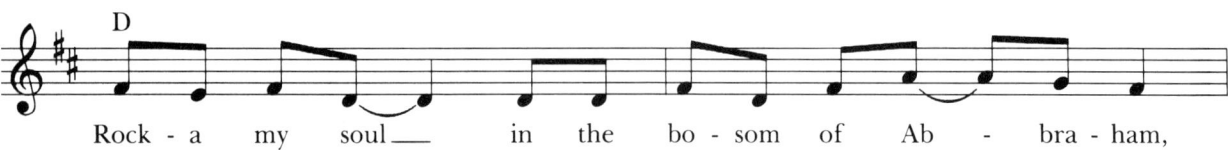

Rock - a   my   soul ___   in   the   bo - som   of   Ab - bra - ham,

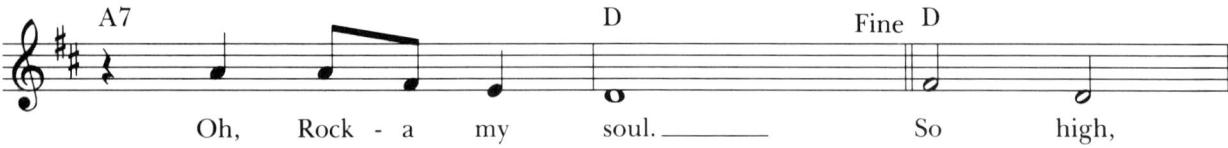

Oh,   Rock - a   my   soul. _____   So   high,

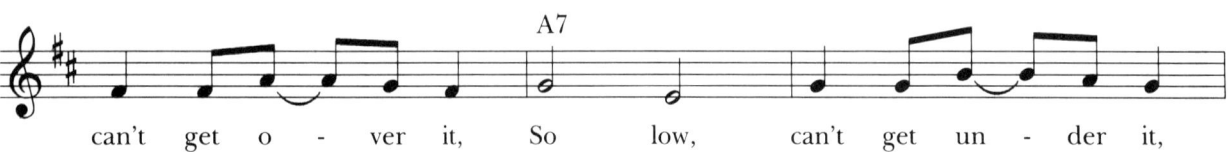

can't   get   o - ver   it,   So   low,   can't   get   un - der   it,

So   wide,   can't   get   'round ___   it,   Must   go   in   at   the   door.

Introducing Song 5:
"Old MacDonald"

Key: G Major
Starting pitch: Do (G)
Count off: 1   2   Ready Sing
              /   /   /   /
Meter: 4
Structure: A
                A
                B
                A
Pitch range: Good for elementary-age children

Song 5

OLD MACDONALD
(A simplified version)

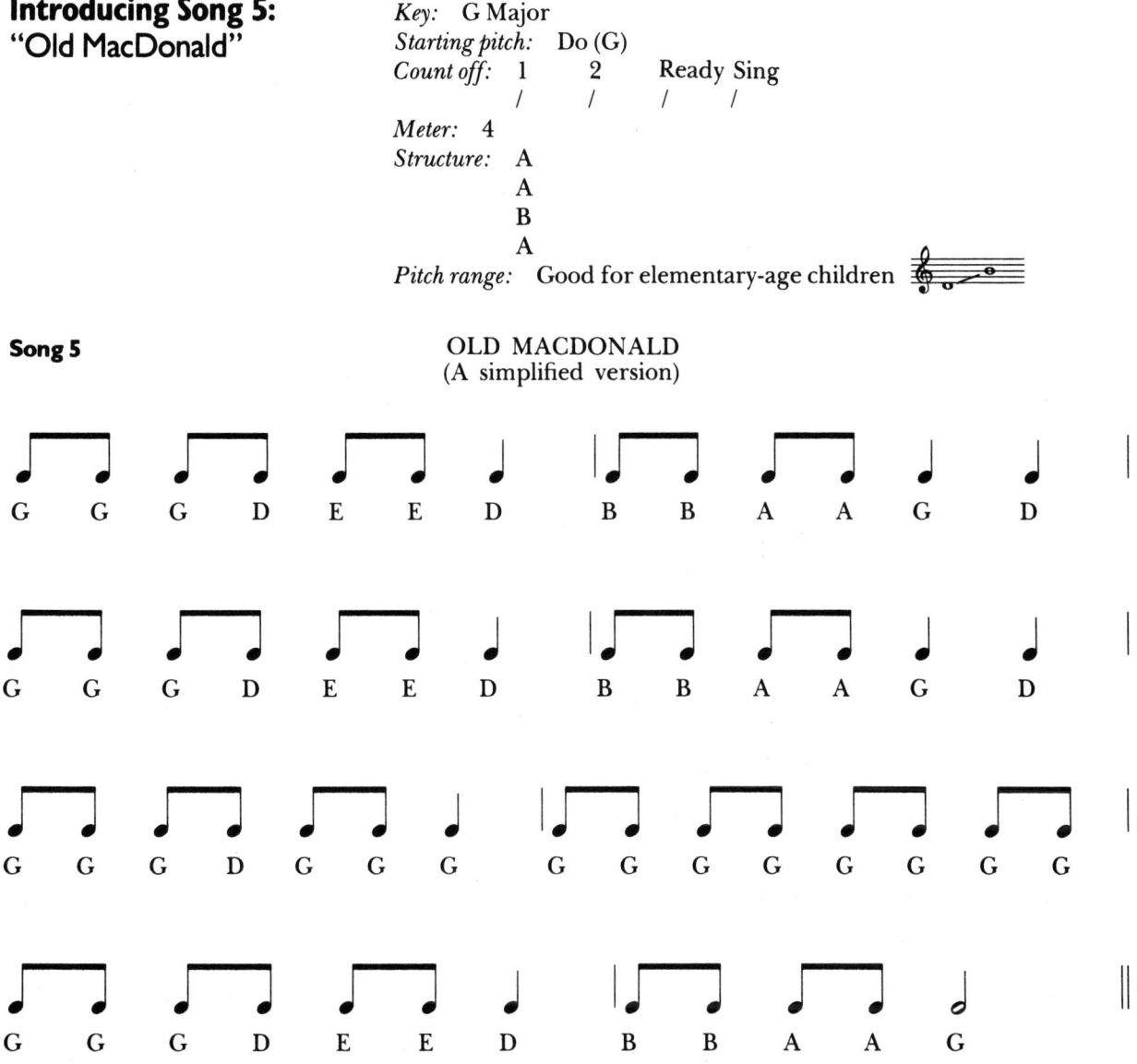

G G G D E E D   B B A A G D

G G G D E E D   B B A A G D

G G G D G G G   G G G G G G G G

G G G D E E D   B B A A G

Introducing Song 6:
"Jolly Old Saint Nicholas"

Key: G Major
Starting pitch: Mi (B)
Count off: 1-2-Ready-Sing
Meter: 2
Structure: A
                B
                A
                B′

Expressiveness: Very happily; lively
Pitch range: Good for elementary-age children

Potential trouble spots: You are probably used to hearing this song at a very lively pace. Therefore, you may be tempted to practice it too fast. A famous music teacher once said, "Practice slowly, then again slowly, and again slowly. Then and only then are you ready to practice it again . . . slowly."

Hint: Notice that the song is written in two ways (on this page and on the next page). Compare how the song looks with and without pitch notation. When practicing any piece of music, always clap the rhythm first (like the first version), then add the pitches to the rhythm (like the second version).

Song 6A   JOLLY OLD SAINT NICHOLAS

Song 6B

JOLLY OLD SAINT NICHOLAS

Jol - ly old Saint Nich - o - las, Lean your ear this way.

Don't you tell a sin - gle soul what I'm going to say.

Christ - mas eve is com - ing soon. Now you dear old man,

Whis - per what you'll bring to me Tell me if you can.

Introducing Song 7:
"Tom Dooley"

Key: G Major (to be playable on the recorder)
Starting pitch: Sol (D)
Possible introduction: G / / / |Am/ / / | G / / / | D7 / / / |
Count off: (last measure of introduction)

        1   2   Ready Sing
        /   /   /   /

Meter: 4
Phrase structure: A
                       A'
                       A'
                       B

Expressiveness: Contemplative
Pitch range: Good for children

Potential trouble spots: Notice that the song is notated two ways. The first way has a simple rhythm pattern; the second way has a syncopated pattern. (Syncopation is discussed in Encounter 11). Pick the version which is easiest for you.

Song 7A

TOM DOOLEY
(A simplified version)

Hang down your head, Tom Doo - ley,   Hang down your head and   cry.

Hang down your head, Tom Doo - ley,   Poor boy, you're bound to ___ die.

Song 7B

TOM DOOLEY

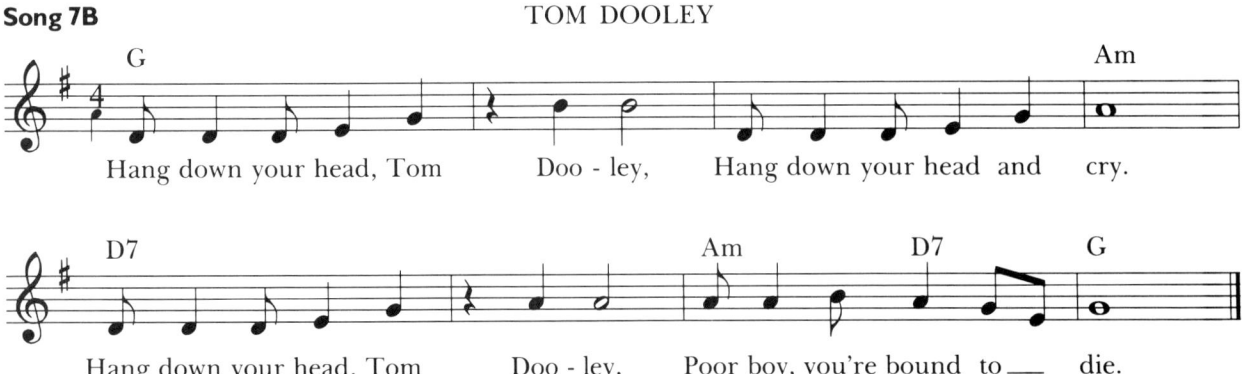

Hang down your head, Tom   Doo - ley,   Hang down your head and   cry.

Hang down your head, Tom   Doo - ley,   Poor boy, you're bound to __ die.

Introducing Song 8:
"Drunken Sailor"

Key: E minor (actually, dorian mode)
Starting pitch: B
Possible introduction: (last four measures)
Em / / / | / / / / | D / / / | Em / / /
Count off: 1 2 Ready Sing
/ / / /
Meter: 4
Phrase structure: A
A'
A″
B
Expressiveness: Energetic
Pitch range: Good for children

Potential trouble spots: In the last two measures, the harmonic rhythm changes. The D chord is only played for four beats this time.

Song 8

DRUNKEN SAILOR

What shall we do with a drunk-en sai-lor? What shall we do with a drunk-en sai-lor?

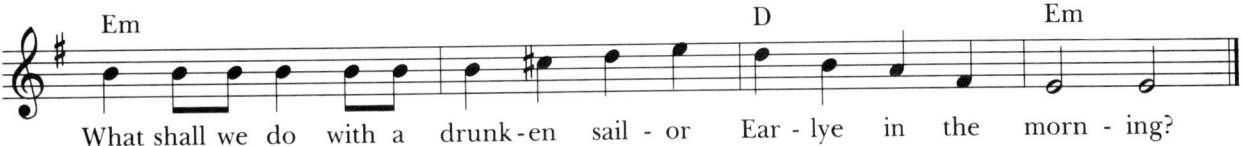

What shall we do with a drunk-en sail - or Ear - lye in the morn - ing?

Introducing Song 9:
"Tom Dooley"

Key: D Major (to be playable on guitar)
Starting pitch: Sol (D)
Possible introduction: D / / / | D / / / | A7 / / / | A7 / / / |
Count off: (last measure of introduction)
           1   2   Ready   Sing
           /   /   /   /
Meter: 4
Structure: A
             A'
             A'
             B

Expressiveness: Contemplative
Pitch range: Low for children

Potential trouble spots: Watch for the unexpected rest at the beginning of the second and sixth measures. The guitar accompaniment does not rest, but the voices singing the melody do.

Song 9

TOM DOOLEY

Chorus

Hang down your head, Tom Doo-ley, Hang down your head and cry.

Hang down your head, Tom Doo-ley, Poor boy, you're bound to — die.

1. Hand me down my banjo, I'll pick it on my knee,
   This time tomorrow night, It'll be no use to me.
   Chorus

2. I met her on the mountain, I swore she'd be my wife.
   I met her on the mountain, An' I stabbed her with my knife.
   Chorus

3. This time tomorrow, Reckon where I'll be,
   Down in some lonesome valley, Hangin' on a white oak tree.
   Chorus

4. I had my trial at Wilkesboro, And what you reckon they done?
   They bound me over to Statesville, And that's where I'll be hung.
   Chorus

5. The limb a-bein' oak, boys, The rope a-bein' strong.
   Bow down your head, Tom Dooley, You know you're gonna be hung.
   Chorus

Introducing Song 10:
"Music Alone Shall Live"

Key: D Major
Starting pitch: Mi (F♯)
Possible introduction: D / / | A7 / / | A7 / / | D / / |
Count off: (last measure of introduction)
　　　　　　1　　　　Ready　Sing
　　　　　　/　　　　　/　　　/
Meter: 3
Structure: A
　　　　　　　A'
　　　　　　　A

Expressiveness: A beautiful round to be performed in a flowing manner
Pitch range: Low for children

Descant

Song 10

MUSIC ALONE SHALL LIVE
Round

Germany

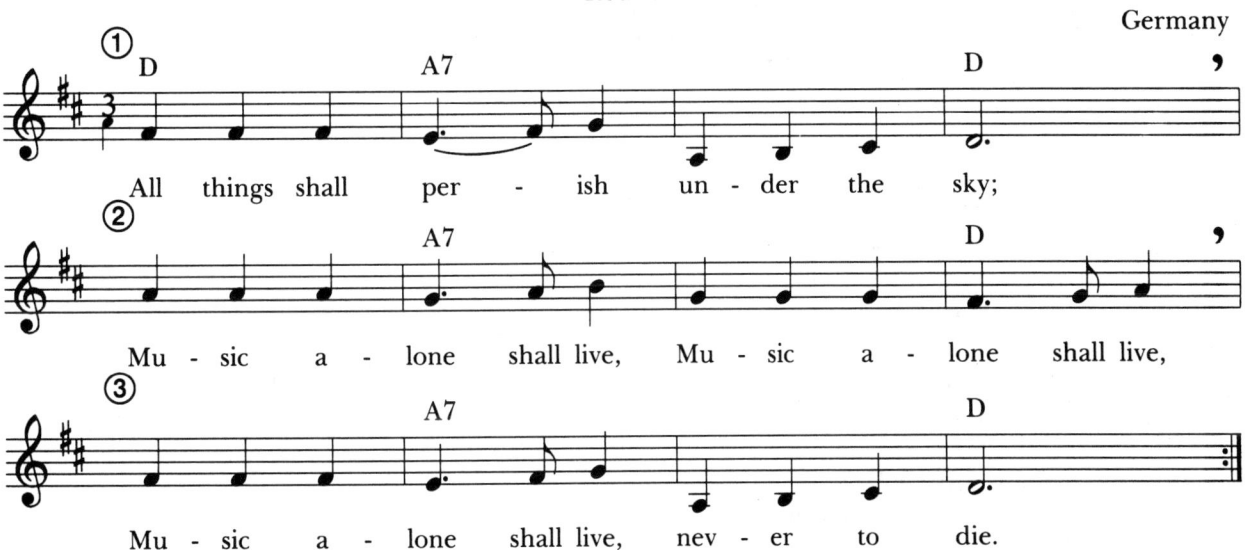

① All things shall per - ish un - der the sky;

② Mu - sic a - lone shall live, Mu - sic a - lone shall live,

③ Mu - sic a - lone shall live, nev - er to die.

MUSIC ALONE SHALL LIVE
Descant

Introducing Song 11:
"Michael, Row the Boat Ashore"

Key: D Major
Starting pitch: Do (D)
Possible introduction: D / / / | Em / / / | A7 / / / | D / / / |
Count off: (first two beats of last measure of introduction)
            Ready   Sing
            /   /

Meter: 4
Expressiveness: Contemplative
Pitch range: Good for children

Potential trouble spots:

Practice the A to F♯ skip on the recorder before beginning the entire song.

Notice how this song begins with Do Mi Sol in order.

Song 11   MICHAEL, ROW THE BOAT ASHORE

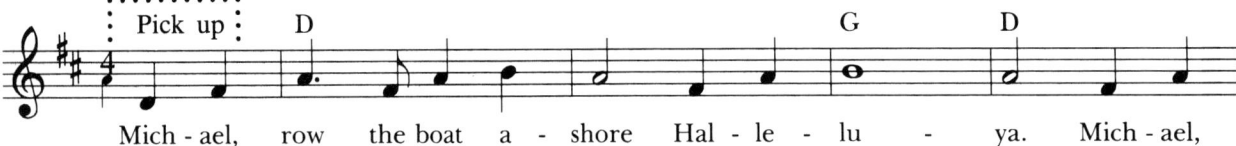

Mich - ael,   row   the boat   a - shore   Hal - le - lu - ya.   Mich - ael,

row   the boat   a - shore   Hal - le - lu - ya.

2. Sister, help to mend the sails . . .
    Sister, help to mend the sails . . .

3. Jordan's river is deep and wide . . .
    Milk and honey on the other side . . .

4. Jordan's river is chilly and cold . . .
    Chills the body but not the soul . . .

PART TWO

Introducing Song 12:
"Over the River"

Key: D Major
Starting pitch: Sol (A)
Possible introduction: Strum on the dotted quarter beat.
D / | G / | D / | A7 / |
Count off: (last two measures of introduction)
1   2 | Ready Sing
/   / | /   /

Meter: $\frac{2}{\cdot}$ (two beats per measure, each beat divided into three parts)
Structure: Notice that lines one and three are musically identical. After you learn the first line you have learned half of the song. Since lines two and four are different from one another, the overall structure, or form, of this song is:

A
B
A   or A B A C
C

Expressiveness: Festive (lively tempo with joyful inflection)
Pitch range: The range of the melody is suitable for all elementary ages. For junior high boys, it may be easier to sing if it is transposed up one or one and one-half steps.

Potential trouble spots: Practice these first!
Guitar: Last two measures—A7 receives only one beat.
Recorder: Measure 14—a change in air pressure is needed to go from A to F♯ to D.

Song 12

OVER THE RIVER

O - ver the ri - ver and thro' the wood, To grand - fa - ther's house we go; ___ The

horse knows the way to car - ry the sleigh thro' the white and drift - ed snow. ___

O - ver the ri - ver and thro' the wood, Oh, how the wind does blow! ___ It

stings our toes and bites the nose, As o - ver the ground we go. ___

161

Introducing Song 13:
"Simple Gifts"

(Fill in any blanks)

Key: _____

Starting pitch: Look at the song to identify which of the following pitch syllables start the song. Circle the correct one, and put the pitch name in the parentheses (for example, Do (D) might be your response).

   Do   Mi   Sol   Low Sol   ( )

Possible introduction: _____

Count off: _____

Meter: _____

Expressiveness: _____

Pitch range: _____

Potential trouble spots: Practice these first! This song has many fast-changing pitches. Practice on the recorder very slowly at first; slowly increase the speed. Notice the half note in measure nine. Also practice measure thirteen until smooth.

Song 13   SIMPLE GIFTS   Shaker Hymn

'Tis the gift to be sim - ple, 'Tis the gift to be free, 'Tis the

gift to come down where we ought to be, And when we find our - selves _ in the

place just _ right 'Twill _ be in the val - ley of love and de - light. When true sim -

plic - i - ty is gained, To bow and to bend we will not be a - shamed. To

turn, _ to _ turn, _ will _ be our de - light And by turn - ing, turn - ing we come 'round right.

Introducing Song 14:
"It's a Small World"

(Fill in any blanks)

Key: _____

Starting pitch: Circle the correct starting pitch syllable identified from the music for this song, and put the pitch letter name in the parentheses.

    Do   Mi   Sol   Low Sol ( )

Possible introduction: _____

Count off: _____

Meter: _____

Expressiveness: _____

In this song the refrain harmonizes with the melody. Try having half the class play the refrain on the recorder while the rest of the class plays guitar and sings the verse.

Song 14   IT'S A SMALL WORLD   Richard M. Sherman
                                                              Robert B. Sherman

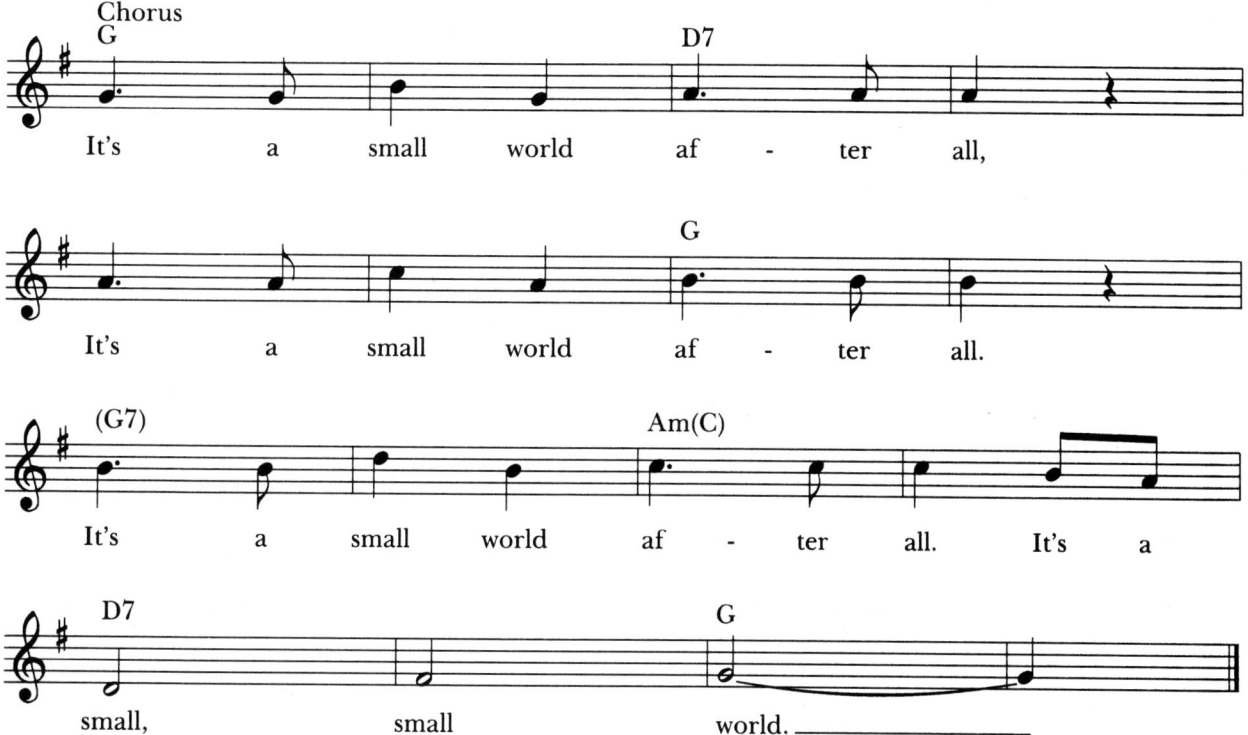

2. There is just one moon and one golden sun.
   And a smile means friendship to everyone.
   Though the mountains divide and the oceans are wide,
   It's a small world after all.

Introducing Song 15:
"Home on the Range"

(Fill in any blanks)

*Key:*_____

Starting pitch: Circle the starting pitch syllable identified from the music for this song, and put the pitch letter name in the parentheses.

    Do Mi Sol Low Sol ( )

Possible introduction: _____

Count off: _____

Meter: _____

Expressiveness: Slightly sentimental

Pitch range: Comfortable for children

Potential trouble spots: Practice these first! The C Major chord may be difficult on the guitar. A minor can be substituted unless the descants are also being performed.

The following are examples of two more difficult rhythms in this song.

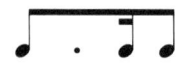

Du (Na) te nee   Du na (nee) te

Song 15

HOME ON THE RANGE

Oh, give me a home where the buf-fa-lo roam Where the deer and the an-te-lope

play;___ Where sel-dom is heard a dis-cour-ag-ing word, And the

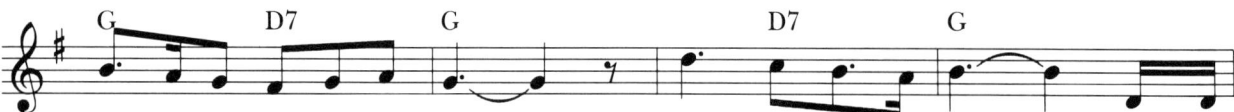

skies are not cloud-y all day.___ Home, home on the range,___ Where the

deer and the an-te-lope play;___ Where sel-dom is heard a dis-

cour-ag-ing word and the skies are not cloud-y all day.___

HOME ON THE RANGE
Descant

Introducing Song 16:
"This Land is Your Land"

(Fill in any blanks)

Key: _____ (Be careful!)

Starting pitch: Circle the starting pitch syllable identified from the music for this song, and put the pitch letter name in the parentheses.

   Do Mi   Sol   Low Sol ( )

Possible introduction: _____

Count off: _____

Meter: _____

Expressiveness: Energetically

Pitch range: Comfortable for upper elementary and older students

Potential trouble spots: Practice these first! Notice that the song starts with three beats of pick-up.

Song 16   THIS LAND IS YOUR LAND

Woody Guthrie

This land is your land, this land is my land,

From Cal - i - for - nia to the New York is - land;

From the red - wood for - est to the Gulf Stream wa - ters; __

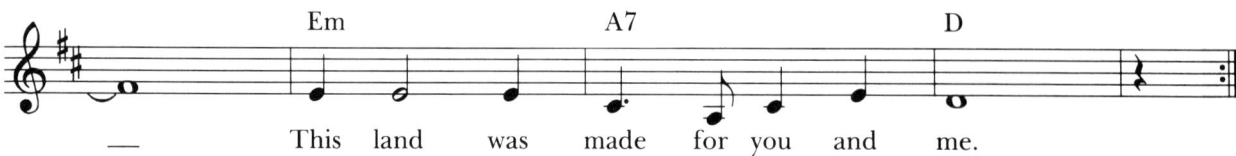

__ This land was made for you and me.

1. As I was walking, that ribbon of highway,
   I saw above me that endless skyway;
   I saw below me that golden valley;
   This land was made for you and me.
   Chorus

2. I've roamed and rambled and I followed my footsteps
   To the sparkling sands of her diamond deserts;
   And all around me a voice was sounding;
   This land was made for you and me.
   Chorus

3. One bright Sunday morning in the shadows of the steeple
   By the Relief Office I seen my people;
   As they stood there hungry, I stood there whistling;
   This land was made for you and me.
   Chorus

4. When the sun came shining, and I was strolling,
   And the wheat fields waving and the dust clouds rolling,
   As the fog was lifting a voice was chanting;
   This land was made for you and me.
   Chorus

5. Nobody living can ever stop me,
   As I go walking that freedom highway;
   Nobody living can make me turn back,
   This land was made for you and me.
   Chorus

6. As I went walking, I saw a sign there,
   And on the sign it said "No Trespassing,"
   But on the other side it didn't say nothing,
   That side was made for you and me.
   Chorus

PART THREE

Introducing Song 17:
"Greensleeves"

Key: E minor
Starting pitch: La of G Major (E), First string on guitar
Possible introduction: Em B7 | Em / |
Count off: 1   2 | Ready Sing
         /   / | /   /

Meter: ⅔ Triple: two beats per measure; beats are divided into three subdivisions
Structure: A A′ B B′ (Note that the B section of the song sounds different because the song switches to G Major for these two lines.)
Expressiveness: Should be performed in a moderate tempo with smooth lines to depict a feeling of longing.
Pitch range: Slightly low for elementary children, but usable. The key of F or G minor might be better for singing, but then it becomes extremely hard to play on the guitar.

Potential trouble spots: Practice these first!

   Recorder: High D on third line has the tendency to be played too loudly, thus detracting from the pretty sound you should try to obtain.

   Guitar: A new chord is needed to play this song on the guitar. If you want to work on this song for guitar, which is beautiful, try either of the B7 chords that follow.

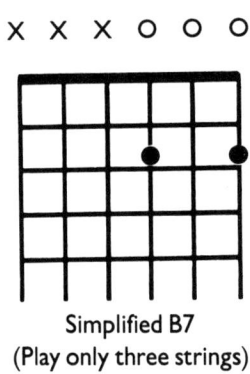

Simplified B7
(Play only three strings)

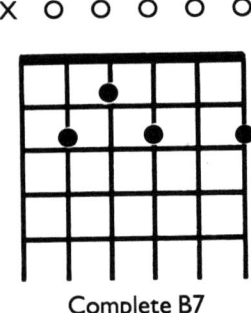

Complete B7

Song 17

GREENSLEEVES

A - las   my love — you do me wrong — to cast me off ___ dis - court - eous - ly And

I   have loved — you for   so   long ___ De - light - ing in ___ your com - pa - ny.

Green - sleeves — was all   my joy _____ Green - sleeves — was my de - light.

Green - sleeves was my heart of gold, ___ And who but my la - dy Green - sleeves.

Introducing Song 18:
"Aura Lea"

(Fill in any blanks)
Key: _____

Starting pitch: Circle the correct pitch syllable identified from the music
for this song, and put the pitch letter name in the parentheses.

    Do Mi   Sol   Low Sol   ( )

Possible introduction: _____

Count off: _____

Meter: _____

Structure: A
              A
              B
              C

Expressiveness: Smooth, restful
Pitch range: Good for elementary or junior high students
Potential trouble spots: None anticipated

Song 18

AURA LEA

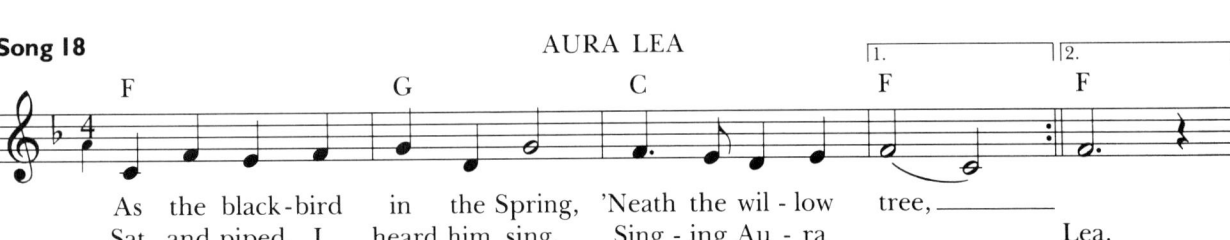

As   the black-bird   in   the Spring, 'Neath the wil - low   tree, _____
Sat and piped, I   heard him sing,   Sing - ing Au - ra   Lea.

Au - ra Lea   Au - ra Lea,   Maid   of   gold - en   hair.

Sun - shine came   a - long with thee, And swal - lows   in   the   air.

Introducing Song 19:
"Coventry Carol"

(Fill in any blanks)

Key: G minor

Starting pitch: La (G), third guitar string

Possible introduction: Gm / D7 | Gm / / |

Count off: _____

Meter: _____

Structure: A
　　　　　　B
　　　　　　C
　　　　　　B'

Expressiveness: Peaceful

Pitch range: Very limited range; good for elementary students

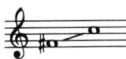

Potential trouble spots: Practice these first!
　　　Recorder: Watch for the B natural at the end!
　　　Guitar: Very difficult, probably beyond your abilities at this time.

Song 19　　　　　　　　　　COVENTRY CAROL

England

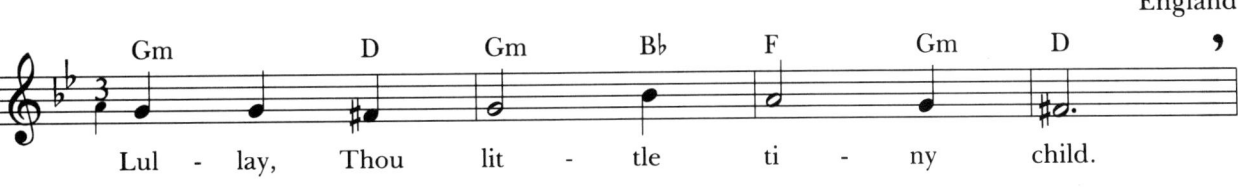

Lul - lay,　Thou　lit - tle　ti - ny　child.

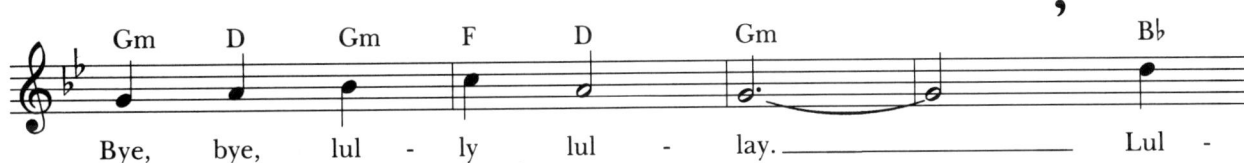

Bye,　bye,　lul - ly　lul - lay._____　Lul -

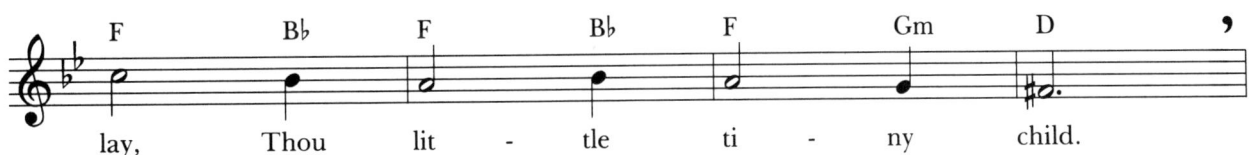

lay,　Thou　lit - tle　ti - ny　child.

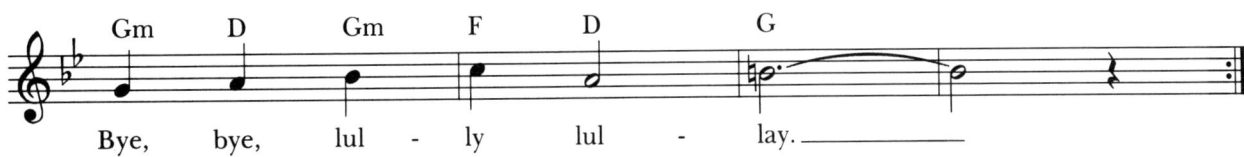

Bye,　bye,　lul - ly　lul - lay._____

Introducing Song 20:
"Theme from Polovetsian Dances"

(Fill in any blanks)
Key: _____

Starting pitch: A, fifth guitar string

Possible introduction: Em / / /

Count off: _____

Meter: _____

Structure: Two similar phrases

Expressiveness: A hauntingly beautiful melody from a large work for orchestra.

Pitch range: Not applicable. No words

Potential trouble spots: Practice these first!

Recorder: Be careful not to attack the high E. Also, remember the first and second ending.

Guitar: None anticipated

Song 20

THEME
Polovetsian Dances

Alexander Borodin

Introducing Song 21:
"Bicycle Built for Two"

(Fill in any blanks)

Key: _____

Starting pitch: Circle the correct starting pitch syllable identified from the music for this song, and put the pitch letter name in the parentheses.

Do Mi Sol Low Sol ( )

Possible introduction: _____

Count off: _____

Meter: _____

Expressiveness: A delightful, carefree love song from the turn of the century. Try to make the sound flowing.

Pitch range: Good for upper elementary-age children. (Watch that first note!)

Potential trouble spots: None anticipated

Song 21

BICYCLE BUILT FOR TWO

Introducing Song 22:
"Five Hundred Miles"

(Fill in any blanks)
Key: _____

Starting pitch: _____

Possible introduction: G / / / | Am / / / | D7 / / / | G / / / |

Count off: (last measure of introduction)

　　　　　　　Ready   Sing
　　　　　　　/　　　/　　　/　　　/

Meter: _____

Expressiveness: Contemplative, sad

Pitch range: Good for children

A beautiful song for a guitar and recorder duet!

Song 22   FIVE HUNDRED MILES

Hedy West

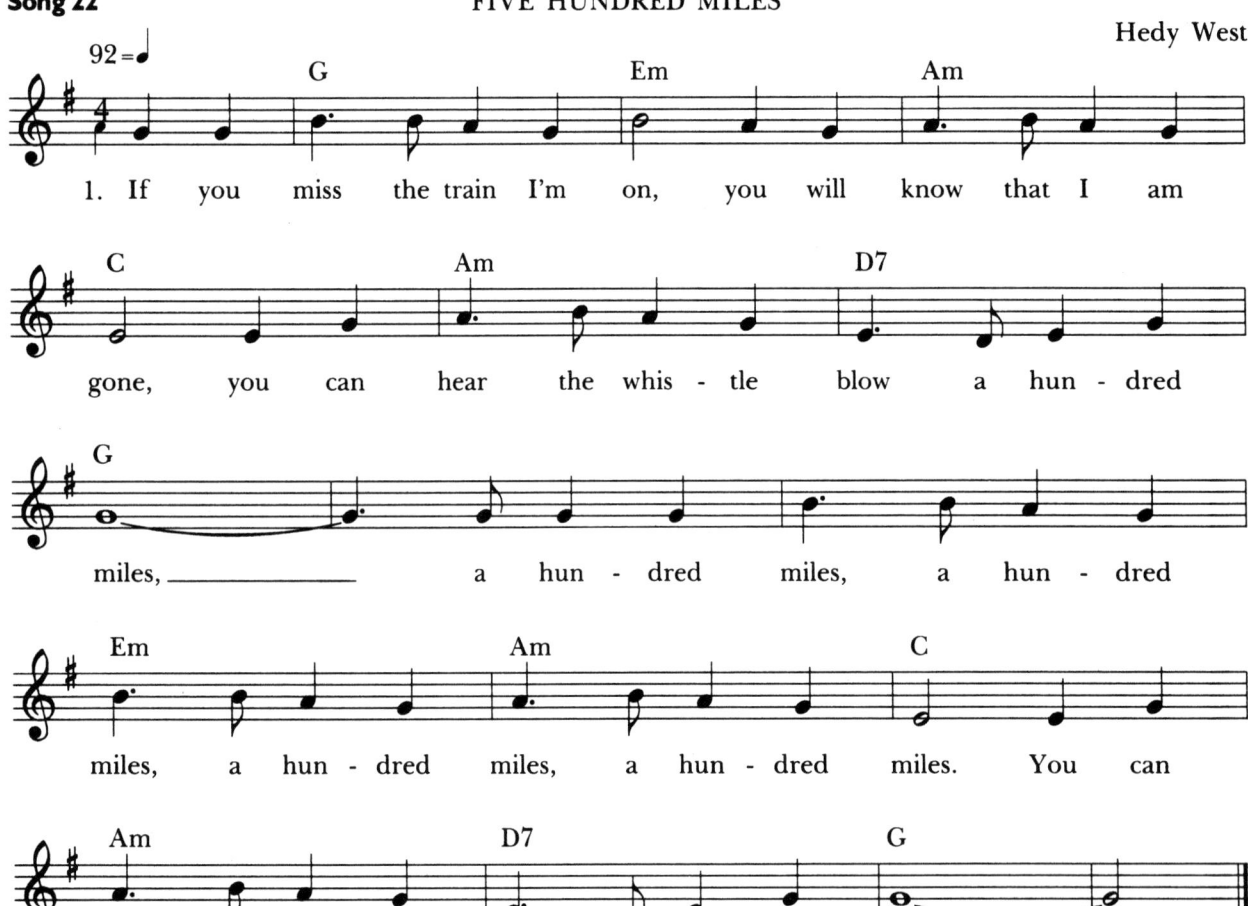

1. If you miss the train I'm on, you will know that I am gone, you can hear the whis - tle blow a hun - dred miles, _____ a hun - dred miles, a hun - dred miles, a hun - dred miles, a hun - dred miles. You can hear the whis - tle blow a hun - dred miles. _____

2. Lord I'm one, Lord I'm two, Lord I'm three, Lord I'm four
    Lord I'm five hundred miles away from home.
    Away from home, away from home, away from home, away from home.
    Lord I'm five hundred miles away from home.

3. Not a shirt on my back, Not a penny to my name.
    Lord I can't go back home this away.
    This away, this away, this away, this away,
    Lord I can't go back home this away.

Introducing Song 23:
"I Love Mud"

(Fill in any blanks)

Key: _____

Starting pitch: Circle the correct starting pitch syllable identified from the music for this song, and put the pitch letter name in the parentheses.

Do Mi Sol Low Sol ( )

Possible introduction: _____

Count off: _____

Meter: _____

Structure: Two parts: Verse/Chorus

Expressiveness: A downright cute song. Have fun with this one!

Pitch range: Great for children

Potential trouble spots: Practice these first!

Watch for the D.C. al Fine.

Guitar: The F chord is fairly difficult; it is included here for those desiring extra challenge. It is much easier simply to play the D7 chord down one fret.

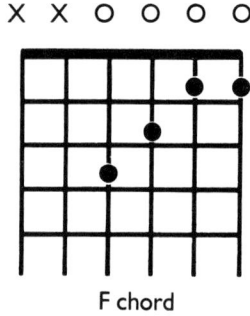

F chord

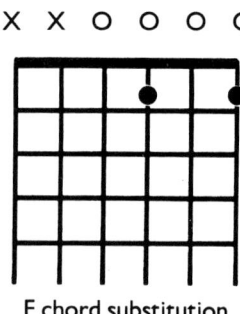

F chord substitution

Song 23

I LOVE MUD

Rick Charette

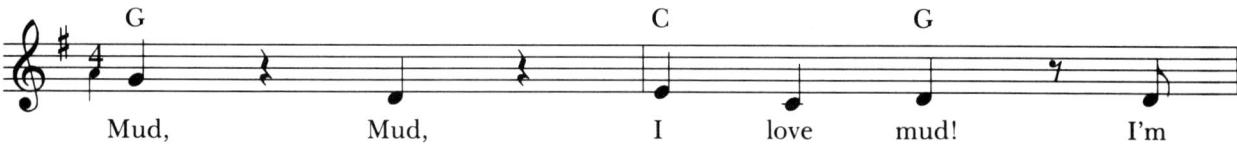

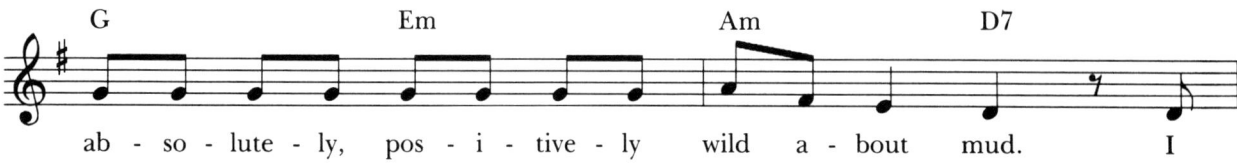

Am   D7   C   G   Fine

Beau - ti - ful,   fab - u - lous,   su - per du - per mud.

G   C   G
Big   Ted - dy   White,   his   clothes were migh - ty   clean.   Went

G   (F)   D7
swimm - ing   in   a   pool   of   mud,   he   made quite   a   scene.   He

G   C   G
start - ed   with   the   back   stroke,   fol - lowed   by   the   crawl.   You

A7   D7   D.C. al Fine
should have   seen   him   swim - ming when   he   heard his   fa - ther   call:

2. Julieanna Root had shiny yellow boots.
   Saw a pool of mud that she wanted to go through.
   She only took two steps. Then she disappeared.
   Nobody's seen her for twenty-five years.
   Chorus

3. Little Rusty Night, he was only three.
   Was working in the mud on his favorite recipe.
   With sticks and bugs and sour milk, it looked like brown ice cream.
   When he started tasting it, he heard his mother scream.
   Chorus

4. Now I would be the last to tell you what to do.
   And when it comes to mud you know it's really up to you.
   So if you can't decide and you're sitting on the fence,
   The most important thing to do is use your common sense.
   Chorus

From the album, *Alligator in the Elevator,* by Rich Charette. Pine Point Record
Company, P.O. Box 901, Windham, ME. Used by permission.

Introducing Song 24:
"We Shall Overcome"

(Fill in any blanks)

Key: _____

Starting pitch: Circle the correct starting pitch syllable identified from the music for this song, and put the pitch letter name in the parentheses.

Do Mi   Sol   Low Sol   (   )

Possible introduction: _____

Count off: _____

Meter: _____

Expressiveness: Convincingly powerful

Pitch range: Good for elementary age children

Potential trouble spots: None anticipated

Song 24

WE SHALL OVERCOME

We shall o - ver - come, _____ We shall o - ver - come, _____

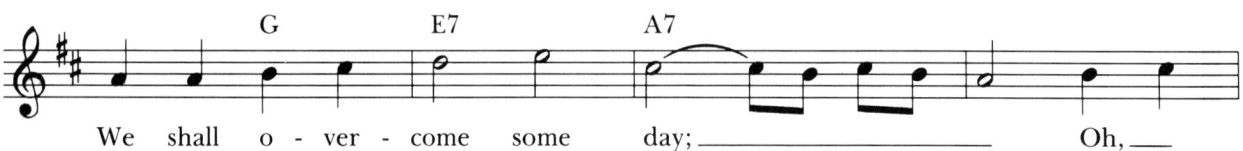

We shall o - ver - come some day; _____ Oh, ___

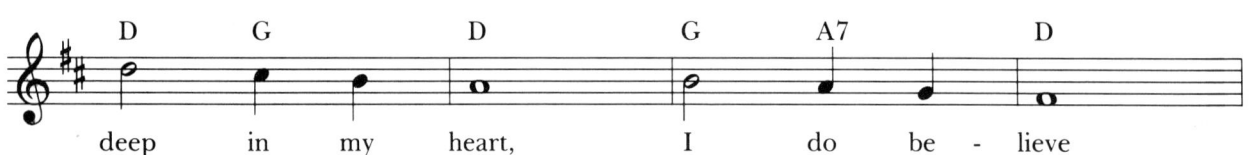

deep in my heart, I do be - lieve

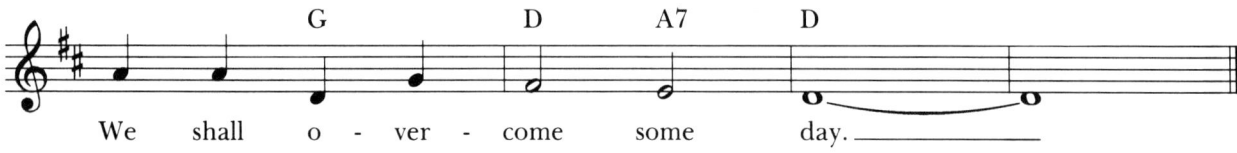

We shall o - ver - come some day. _____

2. We'll walk hand in hand.

3. Truth will make us free.

4. We are not afraid.

5. We shall live in peace.

6. We shall overcome.

Introducing Song 25
"Leaving on a Jet Plane"

(Fill in any blanks)

Key: Use your skill at transposing to try this song in several keys. Which keys are better for playing an accompaniment on the guitar? Which are better for singing? Remember, you must sing the song and accompany yourself in the same key. Can you play this song on the recorder? What key would be best?

Starting pitch: Do

Possible introduction: _____

Count off: _____

Meter: _____

Expressiveness: _____

Pitch range: Depends on key

Potential trouble spots: Be sure to end on a I chord after the third verse. Notice the I chord in parentheses.

Song 25   LEAVING ON A JET PLANE

John Denver

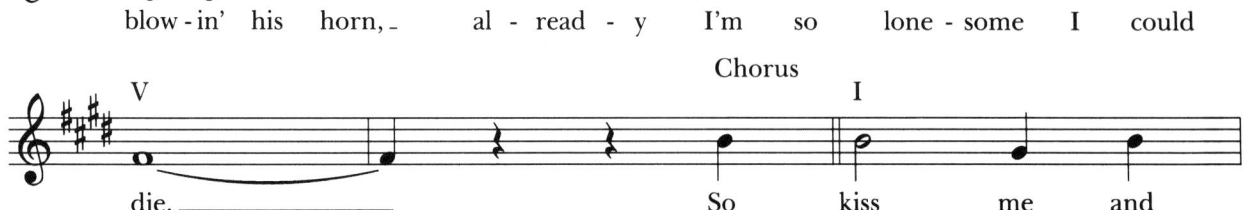

smile for me __ tell me that __ you'll wait for me, __

hold me like __ you'll nev - er let me go, __

__ 'cause I'm leav - in on a jet __ plane, __ don't know when

I'll be back __ a - gain, __ oh babe, I hate to

go. __   2. There's so
                                          3. __

2. There's so many times I've let you down,
    So many times I've played around,
    I tell you now, they don't mean a thing.
    Ev'ry place I go I'll think of you,
    Ev'ry song I sing I'll sing for you,
    When I come back I'll bring your wedding ring.
    Chorus

3. Now the time has come to leave you,
    One more time, let me kiss you,
    Then close your eyes, I'll be on my way.
    Dream about the days to come
    When I won't have to leave alone,
    About the times I won't have to say:
    Chorus

MORE SONGS TO SING
AND PLAY

AMAZING GRACE

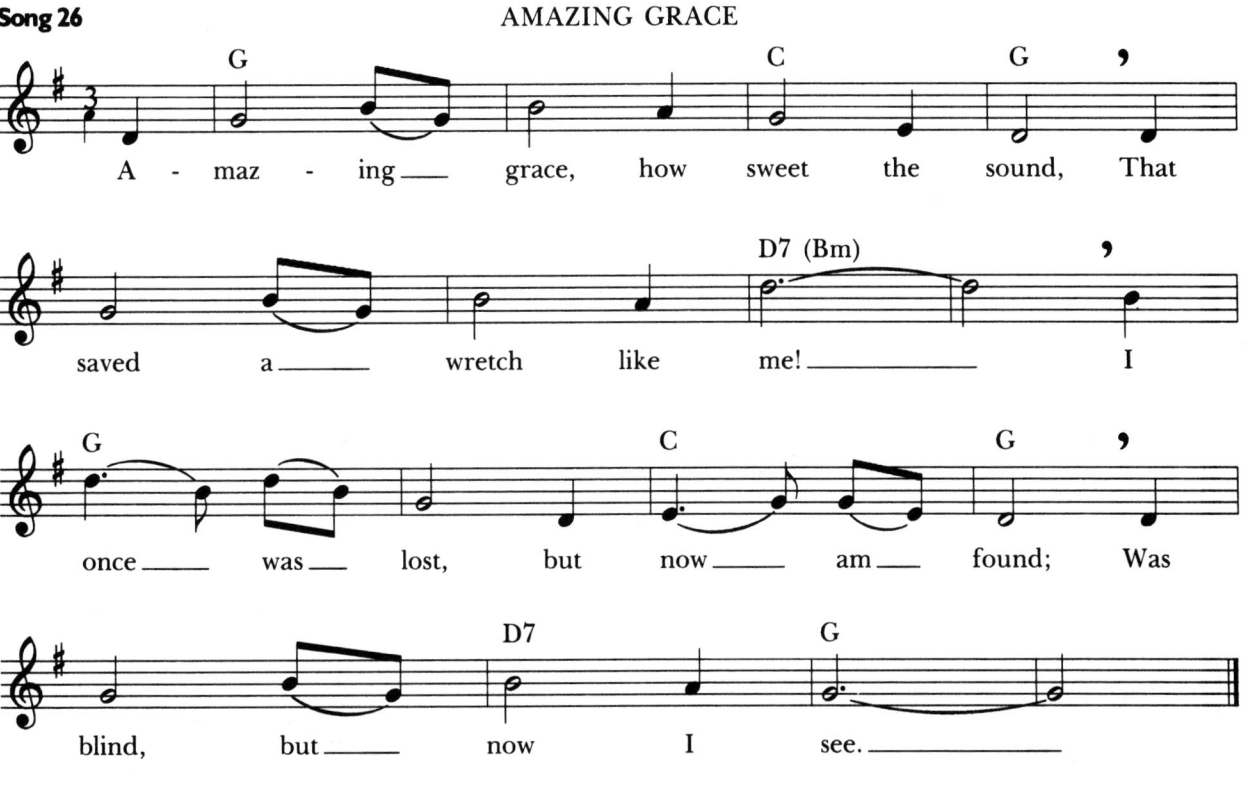

A - maz - ing ___ grace, how sweet the sound, That
saved a ___ wretch like me! ___ I
once ___ was ___ lost, but now ___ am ___ found; Was
blind, but ___ now I see. ___

AMAZING GRACE
Descant

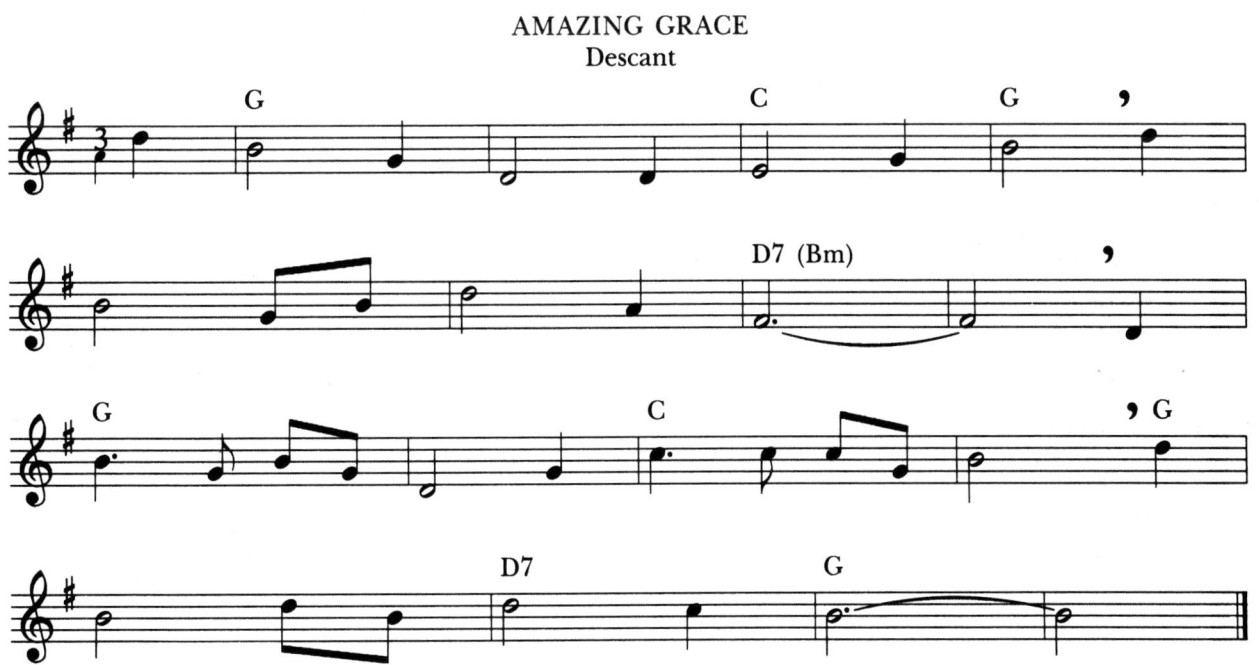

Song 27

SLOOP JOHN B.

So hoist up the John B.'s sails, see how the main sail sets.

Call for the captain a - shore, let me go home; Let me go

home. I wan - na go home. I

feel so broke _ up, __ I wan - na go home. _____

1. We come on the Sloop John B.
   My Grandfather and me
   Around Nassau town we did roam.
   Drinking all night, got into a fight
   I feel so broke up, I wanna go home.
   Chorus

2. The first mate he got drunk,
   And broke in the captain's trunk,
   The constable had to come take him away.
   Sheriff John Sloan, you leave me alone,
   I feel so broke up, I wanna go home.
   Chorus

3. The poor cook he got the fits,
   Threw away all my grits,
   And then he took and ate up all of my corn.
   Let me go home, why don't they let me go home?
   This is the worst trip I've ever been on.
   Chorus

Song 28

DOWN BY THE RIVERSIDE

Song 29

LOVE IS THE MESSAGE

Words and music:
Sylvia Wallach

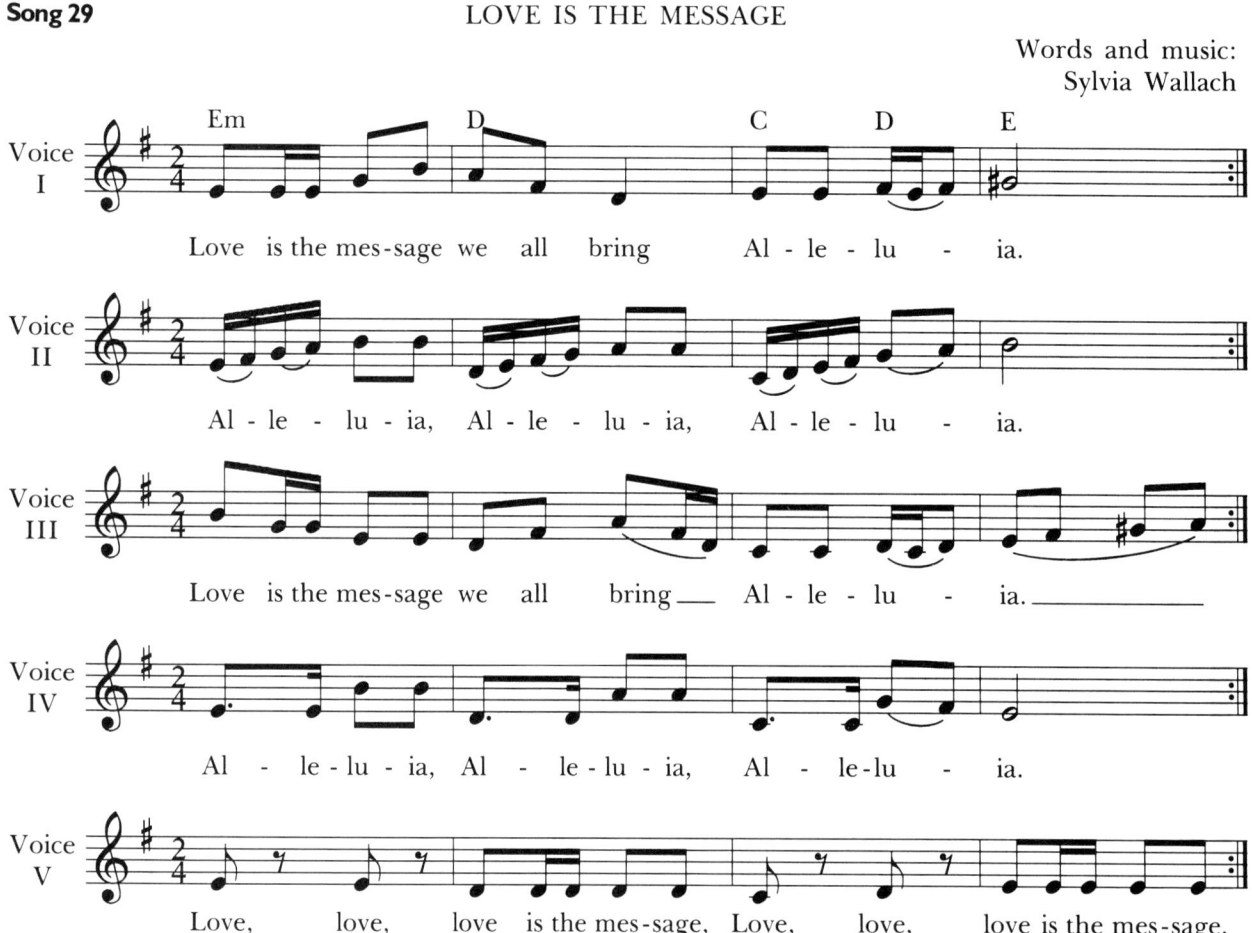

From *Create & Celebrate*. Choral Builder 1, Copyright © 1983 Sylvionics, P.O. Box
60135, Chicago, IL 60660. Used by permission.

Song 30

ROLL ON, COLUMBIA, ROLL ON

Woody Guthrie

1. Green Douglas firs where the waters cut through,
   Down her wild mountains and canyons she flew.
   Canadian Northwest to the ocean, so blue,
   Roll on, Columbia, roll on!
   Chorus

2. Other great rivers add power to you,
   Yakima, Snake and the Klickitat too,
   Sandy, Willamette and Hood River too,
   Roll on, Columbia, roll on.
   Chorus

3. Tom Jefferson's vision would not let him rest,
   An empire he saw in the Pacific Northwest.
   Sent Lewis and Clark and they did the rest,
   Roll on, Columbia, roll on.
   Chorus

4. It's there on your banks that we fought many a fight,
   Sheridan's boys in the blockhouse that night,
   They saw us in death but never in flight,
   Roll on, Columbia, roll on.
   Chorus

5. At Bonneville now there are ships in the locks,
   The waters have risen and cleared all the rocks,
   Shiploads of plenty will steam past the docks, so
   Roll on, Columbia, roll on.
   Chorus

6. And on up the river is Grand Coulee Dam,
   The mightiest thing ever built by a man,
   To run the great factories and water the land, it's
   Roll on, Columbia, roll on.
   Chorus

7. These mighty men labored by day and by night,
   Matching their strength 'gainst the river's wild flight,
   Through rapids and falls they won the hard fight,
   Roll on, Columbia, roll on.
   Chorus

Song 31   HOT AIR BALLOON

Rick Charette

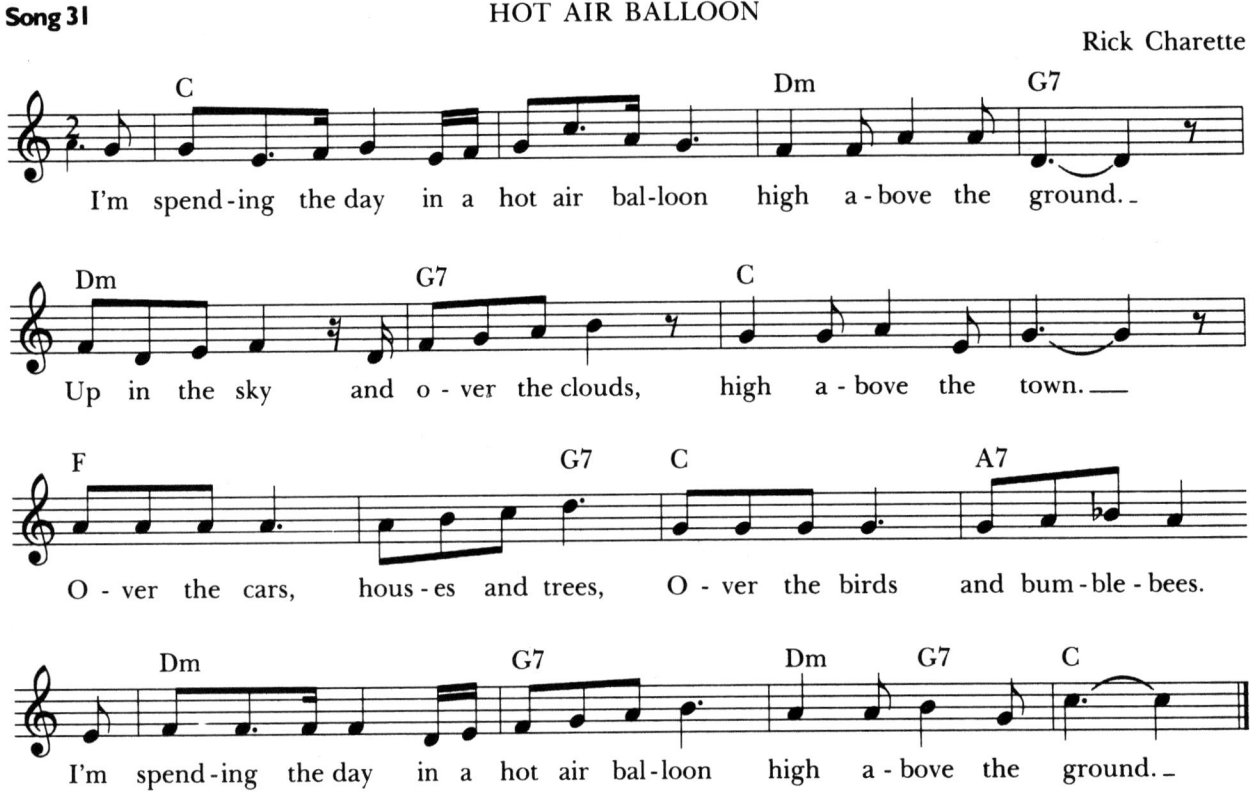

I'm spend-ing the day in a hot air bal-loon high a-bove the ground.

Up in the sky and o-ver the clouds, high a-bove the town.

O-ver the cars, hous-es and trees, O-ver the birds and bum-ble-bees.

I'm spend-ing the day in a hot air bal-loon high a-bove the ground.

Line 3:   Over the playgrounds, over the schools, Over the people and swimming pools.
Over the islands, over the sea, over the sailboats, I'm feeling so free.
Over the hills, in front of the sun, Over the rainbows, this sure is fun.

(Note: Lines 1, 2, and 4 stay the same for each verse.)

This song can be played on the guitar if transposed to the key of D.

From the album, *Alligator in the Elevator,* by Rick Charette. Used by permission.

Ensemble Arrangement:
"Ob La Di, Ob La Da"

Key: _____

Starting pitch: _____

Possible introduction: D   D   D   D

Count off: _____

Meter: _____

Expressiveness: Festive

Pitch range: Good for children

Potential trouble spots: The chord and melody rhythms do not coincide in the chorus section. Suggestion: Practice the chord progression without the melody starting with the word "Hand" at the end of section A. Say the chord name while strumming:

D 2 3 4 5 6 7 8 | A A | G G | D D | A A : ||

Repeat this pattern until comfortable, then add the melody.

Form of this Song:

INTRO | VERSE | CHORUS | VERSE | CHORUS | BRIDGE | VERSE | CHORUS | BRIDGE | VERSE | CHORUS | CODA

Song 32

OB LA DI, OB LA DA

Chorus

Voice

like your face, __ and Mol - ly says this as she takes him by the hand.

Ob la di, __ Ob la da, __ Life goes on, __ La! __ La, __ la, how the

Voice/Recorder

Des - mond has Mol - ly, Mol - ly has Des - mond, La, __ la, how the

Recorders I,II

life goes on. __ Ob la di, __ Ob la da, __ Life goes on, __

life goes on - ward, I'll tell you, Des - mond has Mol - ly, Mol-

La! —— La, —— la, how the life goes on. ————

- ly has Des-mond, La, —— la, how the life goes on. ————

Bridge
Voice

In a cou-ple of years they have built a home, — sweet home, —

Recorder

With a cou-ple of kids run-ning in the yard — of

Des-mond and Mol - ly Jones. ————

2. Desmond takes a trolley to the jewellers' stores,
    Buys a twenty carat golden ring,
    Takes it back to Molly waiting at the door,
    And as he gives it to her she begins to sing.

3. Happy ever after in the market place,
    Desmond lets the children lend a hand,
    Molly stays at home and does her pretty face,
    And in the evening she still sings it with the band.

4. Happy ever after in the market place,
    Molly lets the children lend a hand,
    Desmond stays at home and does his pretty face,
    And in the evening he's a singer with the band.

THE RHYTHM RAPS

THE DU NAY DU CAKEWALK

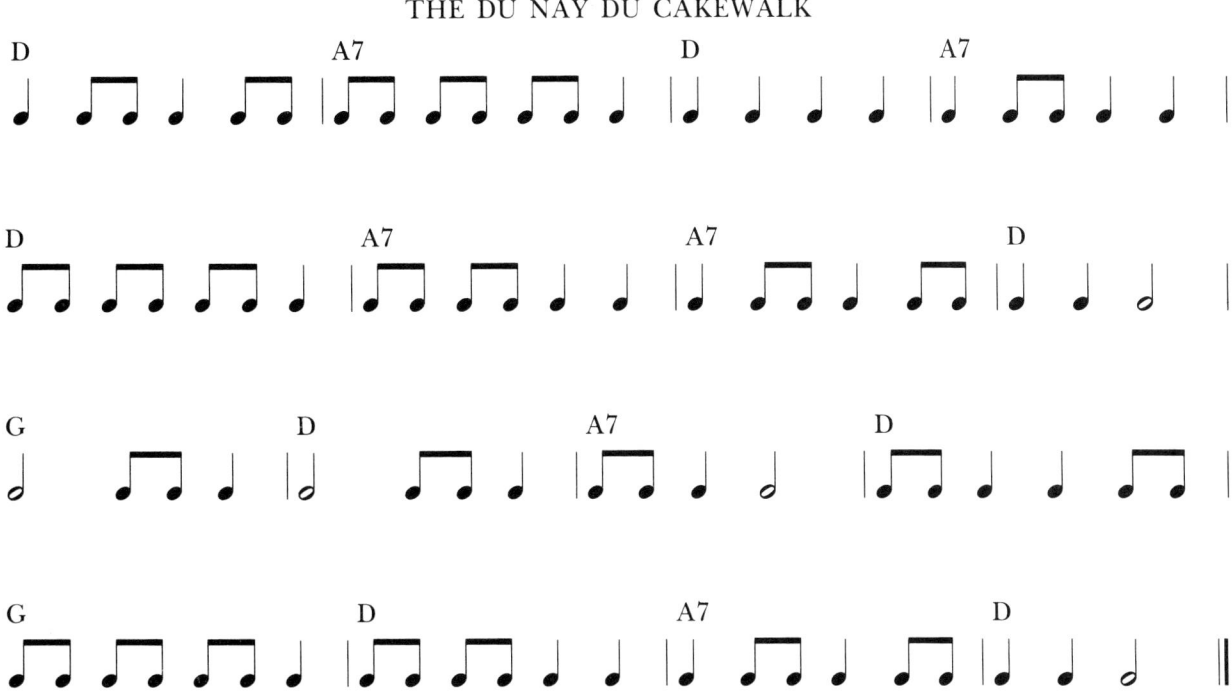

1. Perform these four-measure phrases (lines) in various orders: left to right, diagonally, top to bottom, bottom to top. Try in different tempos.
2. Two or more people can perform their creations simultaneously. Try to experiment with different rhythm instruments or sounds (vocal or percussive).

CREATE YOUR OWN

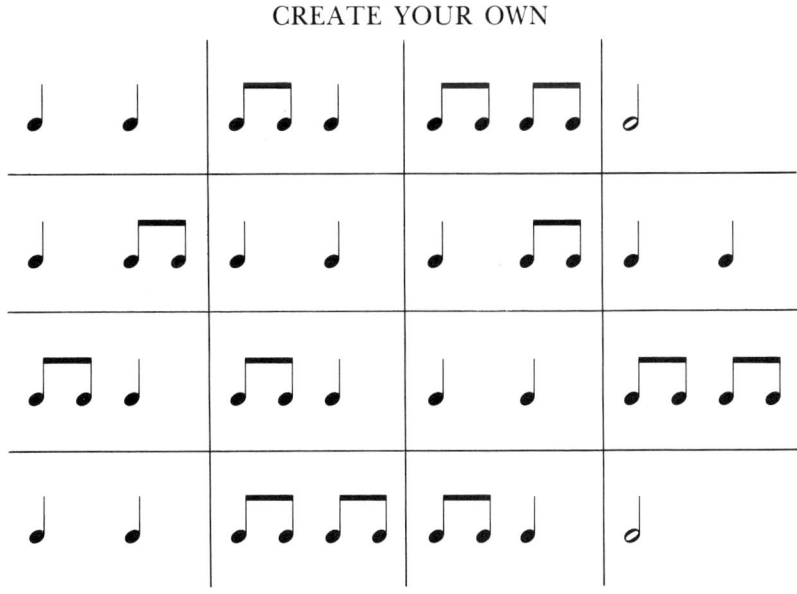

The following examples should be practiced carefully before beginning the "The Du Na Nee Swing." Speak precisely and tap or clap each one several times until you feel comfortable with it.

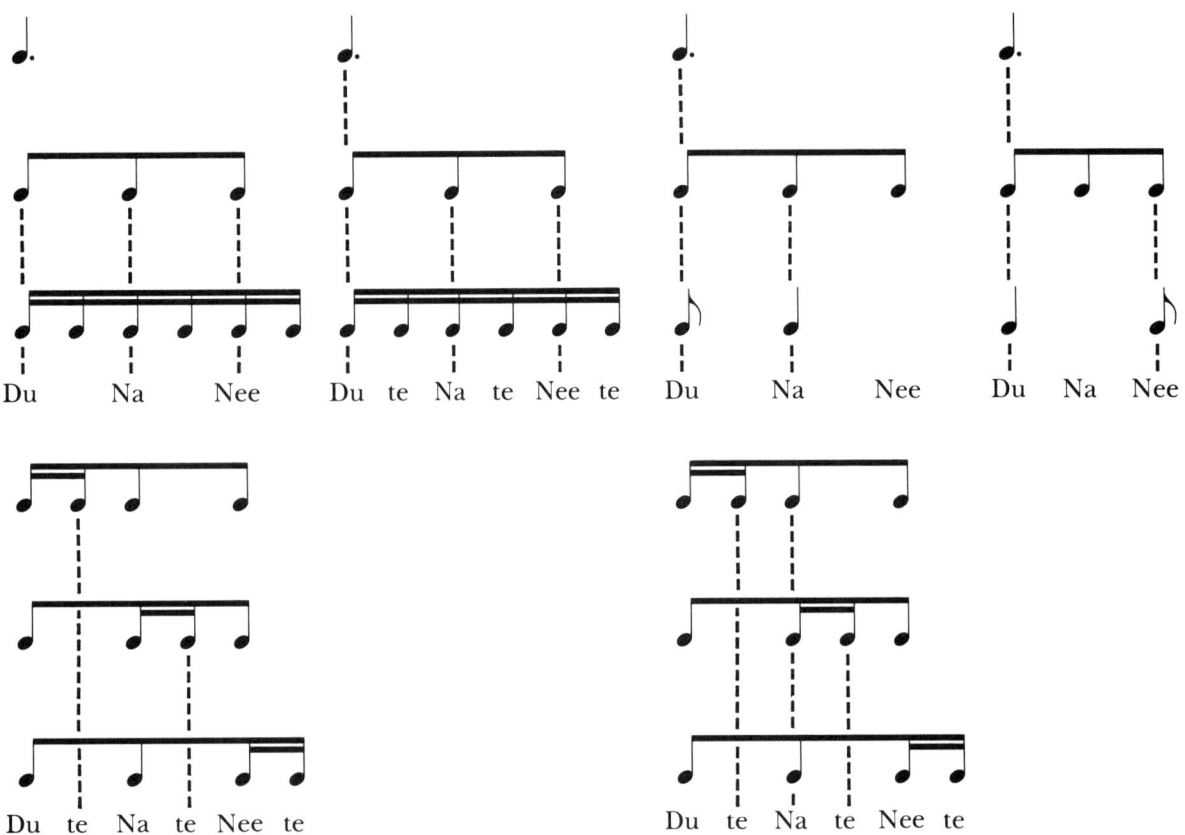

THE DU NA NEE SWING

THE DU TE NAY TE RAP

The following examples should be practiced carefully before beginning the rap. Speak precisely and tap or clap each one several times until you feel comfortable with it.

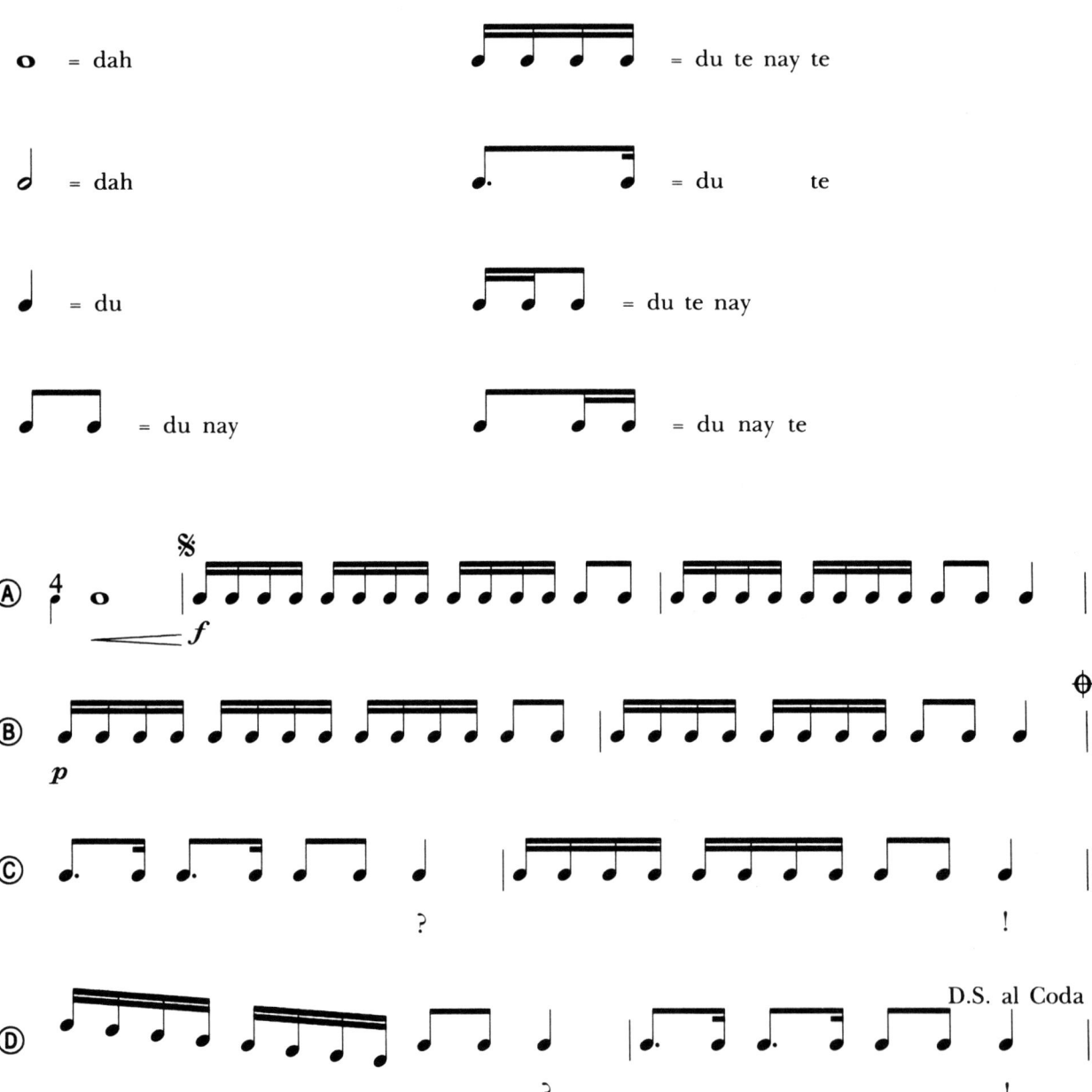

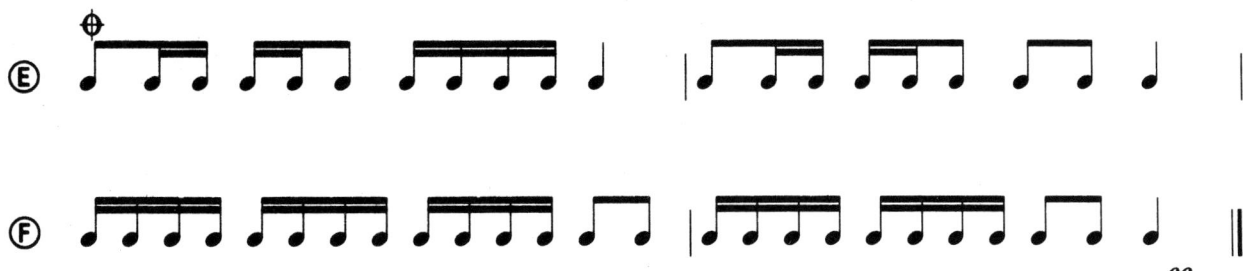

THE WARM-UP BOOK

PREFACE TO THE WARM-UP BOOK

The Warm-up Book* was originally developed based on findings of the most current research in how children learn to sight-sing. It has since been found to be valuable for use with any age student. More than fifty research reports were studied to find the most logical order to introduce pitch patterns, the best visual format for the material, as well as the best manner of presenting the material.

The Warm-up Book has been carefully constructed to provide a sequential plan for learning to sight-sing. Explanations are kept to a minimum; notation is introduced with the pitch syllables Do, Re, Mi, Fa, Sol, La, Ti, Do. Slowly the syllables are removed, leaving only the notation. It is important that the exercises be practiced in sequence, and only one new example should be presented at a time, at least initially. Learning will take place through the sequence and regularity of practice. Similarly, confidence evolves from repeated practice.

Since the student will be practicing the D chord on the guitar during the early part of the course, it would be wise to begin the exercises on the pitch D. Do will be the pitch D.

All of these exercises are in the *Major* mode. It is the authors' belief that students will achieve a stronger sense of accomplishment and confidence by learning selected basic skills and concepts rather than by learning "everything there is to know."

*For detailed description of this book, see Cutietta, Robert. The effects of including systemized sight-singing drill in middle school choral rehearsals. *Contributions to Music Education* 7(1979):12–20.

Warm-up 1

$$\text{Do}^1$$
$$\text{Ti}$$
$$\text{La}$$
$$\text{Sol}$$
$$\text{Fa}$$
$$\text{Mi}$$
$$\text{Re}$$
$$\text{Do}$$

The [1] above the top "Do" indicates this is high Do rather than low Do.

Warm-up 2

$$\text{Do}^1$$
$$\text{Ti}$$
$$\text{La}$$
$$\text{Sol}$$
$$\text{Fa}$$
$$\text{Mi}$$
$$\text{Re}$$
$$\text{Do}$$

(*Note:* Warm-ups 1 and 2 should be sung before *every* one of the following warm-ups.)

Warm-up 3

Do Re Mi Fa Sol Fa Mi Re Do Re Do

Warm-up 4

Do Re Mi Fa Mi Fa Mi Re Re Re Re Re Do

Warm-up 5

Do Re Mi Re Mi Fa Fa Mi Re Do Do Do

The curved line is called a *phrase mark*. It indicates that the notes under it together form a phrase—much like words together form a sentence.

Warm-up 6

Do Re Do Re Mi Re Mi Re Do Re Mi Do

Warm-up 7

Do Re Mi Fa Mi Re Do Do
Re Mi Fa Mi Re Mi Do Do

Warm-up 8

                                      La
                 Sol   Sol   Sol
       Fa   Fa   Fa
    Mi   Mi
  Re   Re
Do   Do

Warm-up 9

Do	Re	Mi	Re	Mi	Fa	Fa	□

Sol	Fa	Mi	Re	Do	Re	Do	□

□ This indicates one pulse (beat) of silence.

Warm-up 10

Do	Re	Mi	Fa	Sol	La	La	□

Sol	La	Sol	Fa	Mi	Re	Do	□

Just for fun: Divide the group in half. One-half sings Warm-up 9, the other half sings Warm-up 10. See what they sound like together.

Warm-up 11

Do	Re	Mi	Fa	Mi	Fa	Do	□

Fa	Sol	Fa	Mi	Re	Re	Do	□

Warm-up 12

Do	Re	Mi	Do	Mi	Mi	Do	□

Re	Mi	Fa	Mi	Re	Mi	Do	□

Warm-up 13

Do	Re	Mi	Do	Mi	Do	Mi	□

Re	Mi	Re	Do	Mi	Mi	Do	□

Warm-up 14

Do	Re	Mi	Fa	Mi	Re	Do	Do

Re	Mi	Fa	Mi	Re	□	□	□

Mi	Fa	Sol	Fa	Mi	Re	Do	Do

Re	Mi	Re	Do	Do	□	□	□

Warm-up 15
Two parts

Part 1	Do	Re	Mi	Fa	Sol	La	Sol	Sol
Part 2	Do	Re	Mi	Re	Mi	Fa	Sol	Sol

Part 1	Fa	Mi	Re	Do	Re	Re	Do	□
Part 2	La	Sol	Fa	Mi	Fa	Fa	Mi	□

First, learn Part 1, then Part 2; then combine Parts 1 and 2; and finally, switch parts.

Warm-up 16

Do	Re	Mi	Do	Mi	Mi		Fa	Sol	Sol	La	Sol	Sol
Do	Re	Mi	Fa	Mi	Sol		Fa	Mi	Re	Do	Re	Do

Songs don't always begin on Do. Here is an example of a song that begins on Mi. Try to sing it. REMEMBER: SING THE ENTIRE SCALE FIRST.

Warm-up 17

Mi	Re	Do	Re	Mi	Mi	Mi	□
Re	Re	Re	□	Mi	Sol	Sol	□
Mi	Re	Do	Re	Mi	Mi	Mi	□
Re	Re	Mi	Re	Do	□	□	□

Warm-up 18

Mi	Fa	Mi	Re	Do	□	□	□
Re	Mi	Fa	Mi	Re	□	□	□
Mi	Fa	Mi	Re	Mi	Fa	Sol	□
Sol	Fa	Mi	Re	Do	□	□	□

Warm-up 19

Sol	Fa	Mi	Re	Do	Re	Mi	□
Fa	Mi	Re	Do	Re	Re	Do	□

Warm-up 20

Sol	Fa	Sol	Fa	Mi	Fa	Sol	□
Fa	Sol	Fa	Mi	Re	Re	Mi	□

After you have learned Warm-ups 19 and 20 *well,* try putting them together to form harmony.

Warm-up 21

Do	Re	Mi	Fa	Mi	Fa	Mi	Fa
Sol	Do	Sol	La	Sol	La	Ti	Do^1

You have now performed warm-ups using all the syllables. From this point on, the syllables will not be spelled out. Instead, only the first letters will appear. Thus Warm-up 21 would look like this:

D	R	M	F	M	F	M	F
S	D	S	L	S	L	T	D^1

Warm-up 22

D	R	D	R	M	R	D	☐
R	D	R	M	F	☐	☐	☐
M	F	S	F	M	R	D	☐
R	M	F	R	D	☐	☐	☐

Warm-up 23

M	R	M		D	R	M
F	F	M		R	D	R
M	R	M		F	S	L
S	F	M		F	R	D

Warm-up 24
Two parts

Part 1	D	R	M	R	M	F	S	☐
Part 2	D	R	M	R	M	F	S	☐

Part 1	D	S	L	T	D^1	☐	☐	☐
Part 2	F	M	F	R	D	☐	☐	☐

Warm-up 25

S	M	S	M	S	M	D	☐
R	M	F	S	F	M	R	☐
S	M	S	L	S	M	D	☐
R	F	M	R	D	☐	☐	☐

Warm-up 26

Sometimes a note lasts longer than one beat. When it does, it is "tied" to a note just like itself, such as M⌢M. In this case Mi is held for two beats but is only sounded once.

D⌢D R M⌢M R M⌢M F S⌢S⌢S

L⌢L S F⌢F M S⌢S⌢S S⌢S⌢S

D⌢D R M⌢M R M⌢M F S⌢S⌢S

S M D F R M D⌢D⌢D D⌢D⌢D

Warm-up 27

S M D⌢D R M F⌢F   M S L S F M R⌢R

S M D⌢D R M F⌢F   D M S S D⌢D⌢D⌢D

Warm-up 28
Two parts

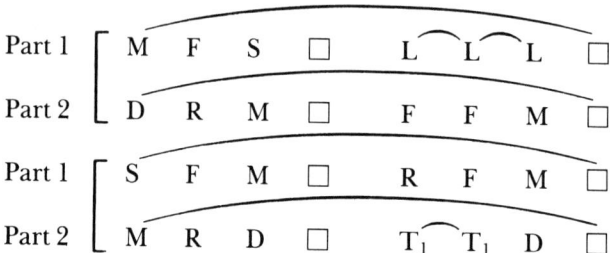

Part 1 ⌈ M F S □   L⌢L⌢L □
Part 2 ⌊ D R M □   F F M □

Part 1 ⌈ S F M □   R F M □
Part 2 ⌊ M R D □   T₁⌢T₁ D □

The subscript ₁ below Ti indicates that this is the Ti *below* the low Do.

Warm-up 29

D R M F   M⌢M⌢M F⌢

S F M R   M⌢M⌢M D⌢

R M F F   M⌢M⌢M⌢M

S F M R   D⌢D⌢D⌢D

Notice where the second and third phrases begin.

Warm-up 30
Two parts

This final warm-up is very difficult. It is included here as a challenge to the advanced group. Good luck!

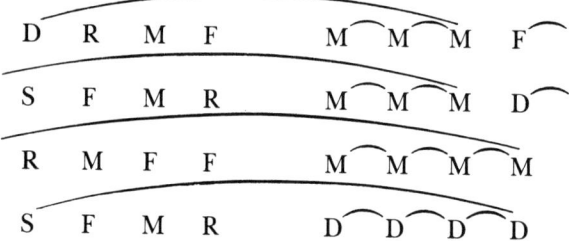

Part 1 ⌈ M⌢M F M F S F M M⌢M F S L⌢L T⌢T
Part 2 ⌊ M⌢M R D R⌢R R M D⌢D R M F⌢F S⌢S

Part 1 ⌈ D¹ D T L L⌢L S⌢S S L S F M⌢M⌢M⌢M
Part 2 ⌊ D⌢D R M F M R⌢R M F M R D⌢D⌢D⌢D

Now that you have learned to sing by syllables, it is important for you to relate the syllables to notes. In some vocal music the syllables are printed under the notes on the staff. Thus, Warm-up 1 would look like this:

All of the following warm-ups will be written this way. While singing, see if you can look at both the syllables *and* the notes.

Warm-up 31

Warm-up 32

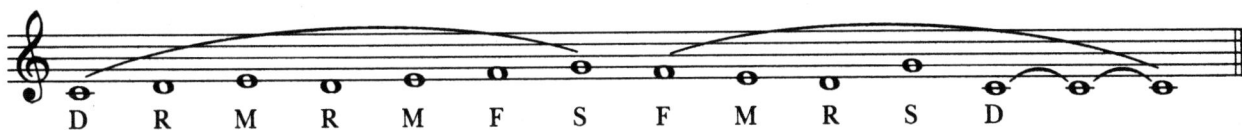

Warm-up 33

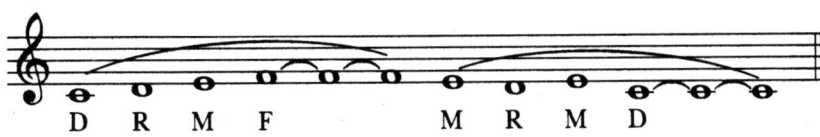

For a note to receive one beat (pulse), it must be colored in like this: ●, and it must have a stem like this: ♩. Each note in Warm-up 34 gets one beat.

Warm-up 34

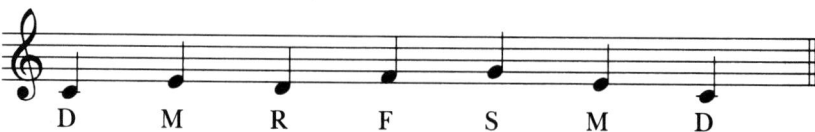

Warm-up 35
Two parts

Try the following warm-up *without* the help of the written syllables!

Warm-up 36

Warm-up 37
Two parts

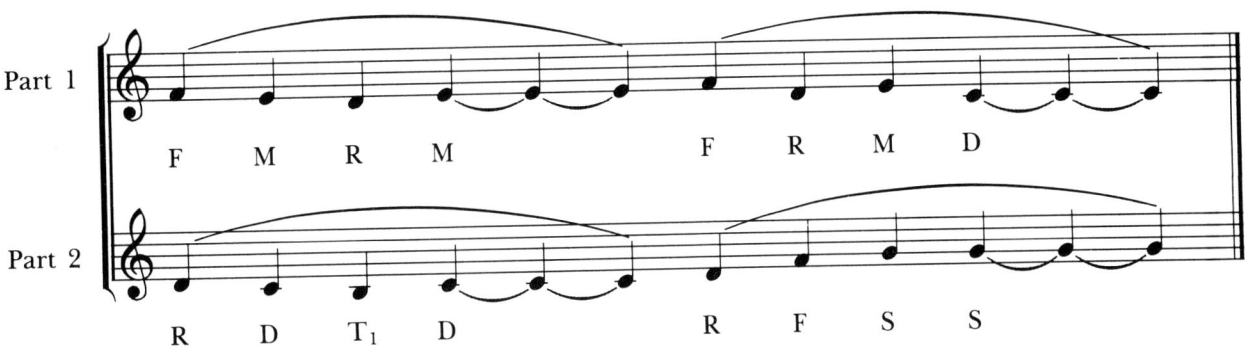

Part 1

F   M   R   M   F   R   M   D

Part 2

R   D   T₁   D   R   F   S   S

"Do" can be on *any* line or space. The location is changed according to the *key signature*.

Warm-up 38

D   R   M   F   S   L   T   D¹
Key Signature

or:

D   R   M   F   S   L   T   D¹
Key Signature

Rule: If Do is in a space, Re is on a line.
    If Do is on a line, Re is in a space.

From this point on, the Do note will always be given before the warm-up, like this:

D

Warm-up 39

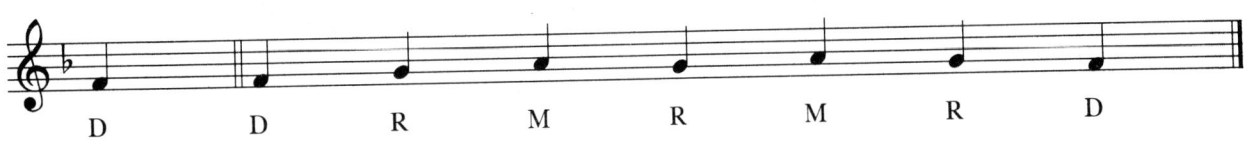

D   D   R   M   R   M   R   D

Warm-up 40

D   D   R   D   T   D   R   M   F   F   M   R   M   R   R

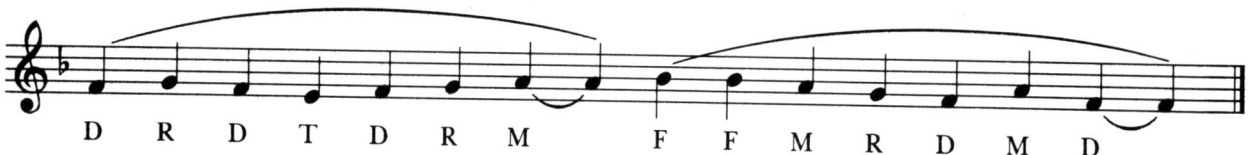

D   R   D   T   D   R   M   F   F   M   R   D   M   D

Warm-up 41

Two parts

Part 1   D   D   R   M   F   S   F   M

Part 2   D   D T_1 D   D T_1 T_1 D

When a note is held for two beats (pulses), it can be written as a hollow note with a stem as follows: ♩ instead of ♩♩.

Warm-up 42

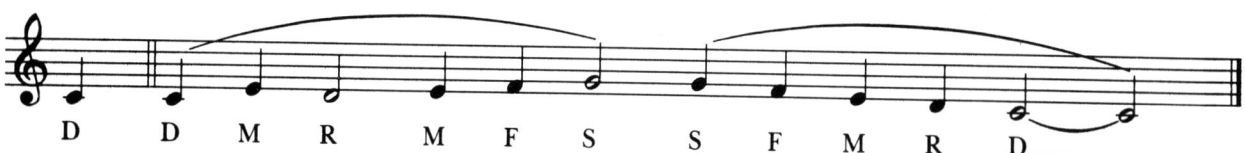

D   D   M   R   M   F   S   S   F   M   R   D_____

Warm-up 43

D M R D R M M M R R R M S S

M R D R M M M M R R M R D

Warm-up 44
Two parts

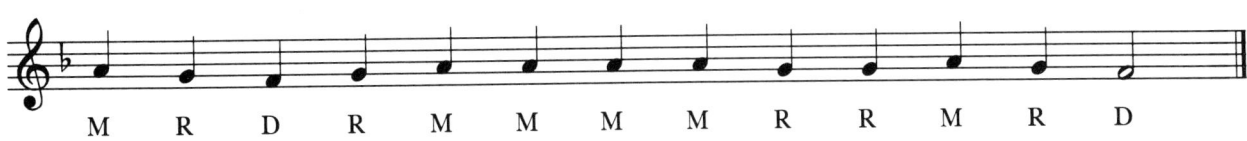

Part 1

D M S F M R M S L L T D

Part 2

D D T₁ D D R D M M M F M

From this point on, the warm-ups will be divided into measures. The number of beats per measure will appear at the beginning of each warm-up as shown in Warm-up 45 and 46.

Warm-up 45
Two parts

Part 1

D D R F M F S F M R D

Part 2

D D T₁ R D T₁ R M R D T₁ T₁ D

Number
of
beats

Warm-up 46

Warm-up 47

Two parts

Warm-up 48

Warm-up 49

Two parts

Warm-up 50

Warm-up 51

Warm-up 52

Two parts

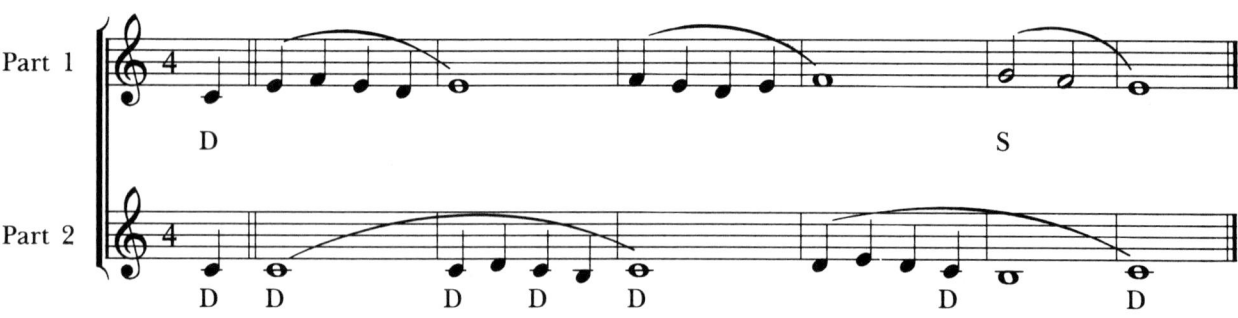

Warm-up 53

Two parts

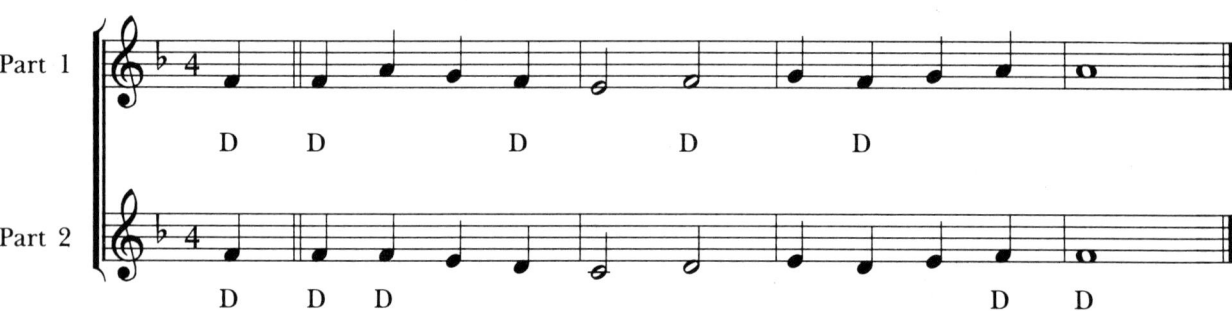

Warm-up 54

Warm-up 55
Two parts

Warm-up 56
Three parts

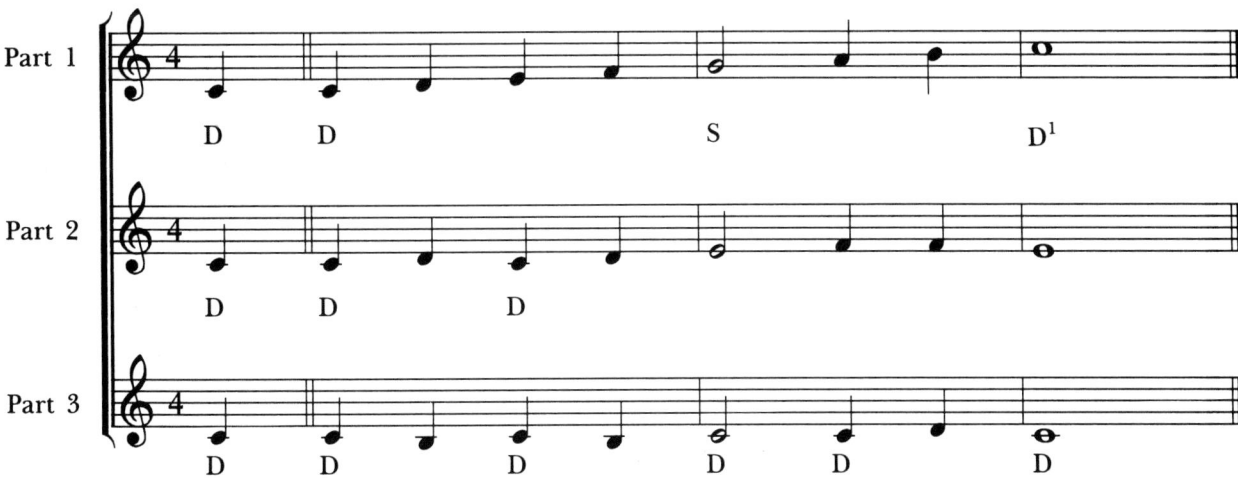

Warm-up 57
Three parts

Warm-up 58
Three parts

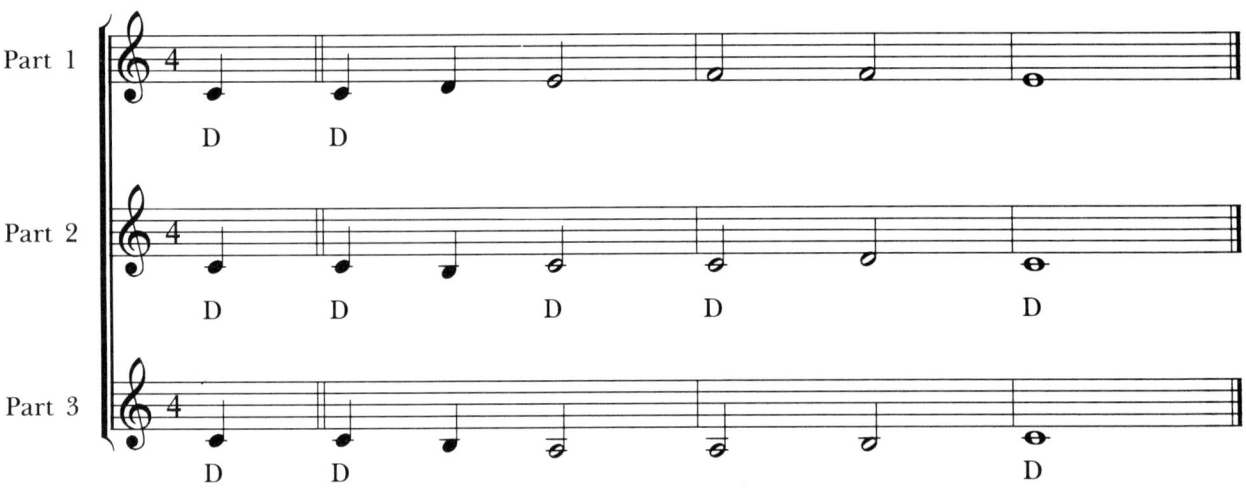

Warm-up 59
Three parts

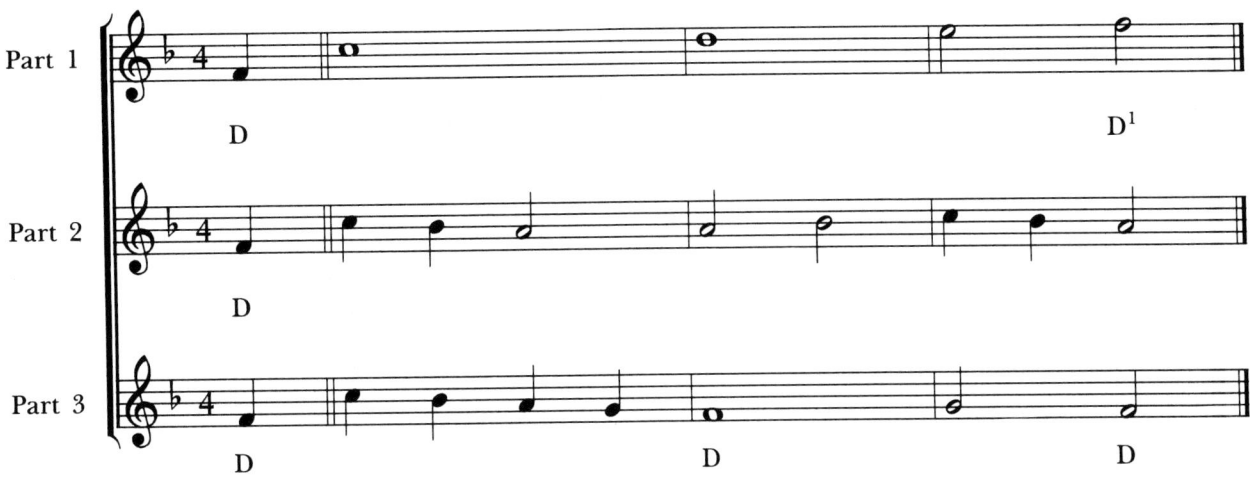

SUGGESTED LISTENING

The following eight musical compositions have been selected to give you opportunities to hear good examples of some of the elements and concepts about music which you are learning in the Encounters. For each composition, a few specific points have been given to help you begin to focus in on the music. Start to become familiar with these compositions right away. Repeated listenings are important, as familiarity brings more enjoyment, awareness and understanding.

Do not try to focus your attention on all the suggestions during one listening. Certain things will become clear to you as you study the Encounters. Enjoy the music, let your attention focus at will, and be open to new awarenesses at each repeated listening. You will probably find that you are hearing many more things than are listed here. Jot them down and in addition, jot down some of your impressions and feelings about the music.

These selections are quite well known, therefore you should be able to find recordings of them in a college or public library.

Johann Strauss, THE BLUE DANUBE WALTZ

Focus your attention on the following:

1. A long introduction. How does it develop? What is its role in the overall composition?
2. Triple division of the beat.
3. Gradual tempo changes: accellerando and ritard. Follow the steady beat.
4. Slight changes of tempo at the beginnings and ends of phrases: rubato.
5. Pick ups in the melody.
6. DO MI SOL melody pattern.
7. The development of the melody.
8. The coda. When does it begin? What musical material is in the coda?

Two Lute Pieces from the Renaissance

Angel Records S-36019 "In the Classic Style" 1968
Focus your attention on the following:

1. A. Triple division of the beat.
   B. The structure of the composition: ABA.
   C. The syncopation at the beginning of the B section: an accent which falls on a weak beat of the measure.
   D. Ritard at the end.

2. A. Repeated bass pattern: an ostinato pattern.
   B. Triple division of the beat.
   C. Simple coda; interesting ending.

Pachelbel, CANON

Focus your attention on the following:

1. Bass line, called a ground bass, acts as an ostinato. The ostinato, which is very short, is the main melody. How can a short melody, such as this one, be used over and over, yet develop into an interesting composition?
2. The countermelodies as they enter, one at a time. This layered effect is an effective way of arranging an ensemble performance. Try to focus on individual lines, or countermelodies as the piece progresses.
3. The particularly apparent relationship of note values: halves, quarters, eighths, and sixteenths.
4. Recurring rhythm patterns easily detected.
5. The bass line ostinato (or ground bass) which forms the basis for the following chord progression. Besides playing these chord roots on the recorder, the complete chords may be played in a recorder or bell ensemble.
   ‖: I   V   vi   iii   IV   I   IV   V   :‖

Copland, SIMPLE GIFTS from "Appalachian Spring"

Focus your attention on the following:

1. The melody and accompaniment.
2. The power of interpreting a melody effectively. In this composition, the composer has chosen various ways to interpret this melody with effective changes in tempo, dynamics and instrumentation.
3. The interpretation of the melody is by a solo instrument. The accompanying melody is like a descant.
4. The tempo changes within one statement of the theme as well as from one statement to another. In order to realize the full effect of the tempo changes, try to finger the first phrase of the melody on the recorder each time it occurs in the music.
5. The dynamic changes within one statement of the theme as well as from one statement to another.
6. The variety of instrumentation and instrumental effects.
7. The background chords which comprise the harmony.
8. The interesting interludes between the various statements of the theme.

Smetana, DANCE OF THE COMEDIANS from "The Bartered Bride"

Focus your attention on the following:

1. Unusually short introduction.
2. Sixteenths in duple meter.
3. Effective use of accents.
4. The expressive qualities: dynamic contrasts, swells (crescendo and decrescendo).
5. Use of repetition to unify as well as contrast the different sections of the composition.
6. Form (or structure) of the composition. The form is called a rondo: A B A C A D A Coda. Notice the use of a solo instrument in one section. Can you identify the instrument and the section?
7. An extended pattern of I and V chords in parts of the long coda: I V I V I V I.

Vaughn-Williams, FANTASIA ON GREENSLEEVES

Focus your attention on the following:

1. Melody in a minor mode.
2. Harmony in the accompaniment pivots back and forth between minor and major chords.
3. Legato sound.
4. A descant-like part played on the violin.
5. Triple division of the beat.
6. Contrasting variations of the theme, from full orchestra to solo line melody.
7. Variations in accompaniment styles: from solid chords to broken chords.
8. Expressive qualities, including many possibilities of dynamics and tempo changes.

Joplin, THE ENTERTAINER

Focus your attention on the following:

1. Melody and harmony.
2. Duple division of the beat; strongly detailed in the accompaniment part.
3. Syncopation; especially one recurring pattern: eighth, quarter, eighth.

Prokofiev, LOVE OF THREE ORANGES from "The Three Cornered Hat"

Focus your attention on the following:

1. Introduction; its role and relationship to the whole piece in terms of the musical material used.
2. Use of percussion instruments.
3. Duple division of the beat.
4. Recurring rhythm patterns.
5. Use of dynamics, especially the use of crescendo and contrasting dynamics.
6. The form (structure) of the composition. How many parts are there? Are any parts similar? Is the form of this composition familiar to you?

INDEX